Louis Cohen, PhD

THE TWO ROOT CAUSES OF
INCOME INEQUALITY
AND A
PRACTICAL SOLUTION

A practical way the middle class can
get the political and economic power necessary
to end income inequality and ensure they get
their fair share of American prosperity

Dedicated to the Internet,
without which this book
would not have been started.

Contents

About the Author   6

Acknowledgments   7

Introduction   9

Part I. Income Inequality and Poor Growth in the New *Stock Price Economy*   13

1. The Two Root Causes of Income Inequality   14
2. The Root Cause of the US Economy's Chronically Poor
   Growth since the Great Recession   36
3. Why Are Corporate Profits and Stock Prices Soaring
   Despite a Weak Economy?   42

Part II. Taxes   45

4. Ten Tax Myths That Make the Rich Richer   46
5. Do Half of Americans (Romney's 47%)
   Really Pay No Taxes?   55
6. How the Wealthy Have Dominated the Tax Cuts   58

Part III. American Attitudes toward Big Government Programs   61

7. Does the Government Subsidize Social Security?   62
8. How Do Americans Really Feel about Big
   Government Programs?   70

Part IV. How to Measure the New
Stock Price Economy   **81**

  9. New Economic Measurements for the New
     Stock Price Economy   82
  10. Who Does the Economy Work for Today?
      Who Should It Work for?   90
  11. Are the Stock Market Indexes Good Measures
      of the Health of the American Economy?   92

Part V. How the American People Are
Misled about Their Economic Situation   **95**

  12. Political and Economic Terms That Lie   96
  13. "Flag-Waving" Patriotism versus
      "Economic" Patriotism   112

Part VI. Some Possible Solutions   **119**

  14. A Permanent Jobs Department   120
  15. US Workers Need Representation in
      Negotiations with Management   131
  16. Vital: A Middle-Class Organization   139
  17. What Would the Middle-Class Organization Do?   146

Bibliography   152

About the Author

Louis Cohen's undergraduate work was in statistics at the City College of New York, followed by a PhD in psychology at New York University. He taught statistics for a few years and gave seminars to clients, and published a dozen journal articles on the research techniques he developed. He then worked as president and principal of a large market research company for 11 years.

When Dr. Cohen realized that he would rather do research than serve as president, he sold his interest in the company and started a small research company, Louis Cohen Research, which he ran for 20 years, doing the lion's share of the research projects himself. Clients included such major companies as Johnson & Johnson, NBC, Bristol-Myers, Westinghouse Broadcasting, and RJR Foods.

Cohen has been a news junkie even longer than a market researcher, and in his retirement devotes his work to timely issues like Income Inequality, healthcare, and entitlements.

Acknowledgments

Lisa Stark pushed me all the way (but nicely!). She was passionate about my ideas, encouraged me to develop them, and gave me good feedback. Lisa also took charge of the book's production.

My son, Alan Cohen, gave me the big idea that a nonprofit, nonpolitical organization for the middle class and other ordinary Americans would have the power to end income inequality and ensure that they get their fair share of American prosperity in the same way that AARP has made sure that seniors get their due—and there are many more middle-class Americans than there are seniors.

James Gray King was my computer maven and a whole lot of other things, including getting the manuscript ready for publication. He also aided me greatly in the book's development.

Dr. Ed Wolff, a professor of economics at New York University. A couple of months into my research, I wanted to get a reaction to my work thus far, Dr. Wolff, experienced in the area of income inequality, said that he liked what I had done, and encouraged me to go ahead with my analysis. I got the feeling that a book could be very useful if I did a good job.

Diego Vainesman, Design Director of 40n47 Design, Inc., did the final design and layout for the book and cover. The book looks much the better for his work.

Gillian McGarvey, editor and owner of Wheelhouse Editorial, did the final edit, fact check, and created the bibliography. If the book looks professional, it's her fault.

I also gave an early draft of the manuscript to Craig Rose, his wife Barbara Rose, and Hilde Jaffe, who read it and made comments that were very useful.

I won't vote for Hillary Clinton, but I agree with the title of her book—*It Takes a Village.*

Introduction

This didn't start out as a book. It began as a research article on the currently hot issue in political economics, Income Inequality. The article led me to research further why the US has had such a chronically poor economy since the Great Recession, which in turn led me to research why the stock market is soaring despite a weak economy. In doing so, I believe I have learned the root cause of these issues and have even arrived at some good ideas on how to solve these problems. I continued to research until I had written more than a dozen research studies on recent important economic and political issues. When at last I studied my results, it turned out that all the research papers related to issues of interest to the middle class—both why and how it has eroded.

I was motivated to research and write the book because I was dissatisfied with the explanations that earlier research has come up with on such subjects as Income Inequality, erosion of the middle class, and a good number of other issues. So I thought I'd make an attempt to answer these questions using the research and thinking techniques I used throughout a career of more than thirty years in commercial research.

The content of this book derives from more than 100 books I have read on the subjects covered here and over 1,000 articles, polls, census data, etc. from the Internet. The book is divided into six sections, with several chapters per section. I based each chapter on a separate research paper.

My main objective for this book was to find the root causes of the Income Inequality we face today and to turn it back to the Income Equality of the three-and-a-half decades following World War II (before the Reagan administration). When we had Income Equality, the five quintiles in income (in chunks of 20 percent) had very similar rates of income increase. Also, in the three-and-a-half decades of Income Equality, we generally experienced good economic times and built the largest middle class in the history of the world.

I thought it would be worthwhile to describe some of the techniques I used from my work in commercial research that turned out to be useful in this research:

1. Solutions, Not Just Problems

In my commercial research, I never wanted to simply present the problems of a client's product or service, whether he was a researcher, the Research Director, a marketing guy, or his boss, the Marketing Director. I found that one of the most successful ways to reach the underlying cause of a problem I was researching was to use the "root causal problem technique and thinking." I discovered that if I found the root cause of the problem, it explained other surrounding problems. Also, it often led to finding a possible solution to the problem my client hired me to research. On the other hand, I found that if I didn't find the root cause of the problem, chances were that I wouldn't solve the client's problem.

I described this technique and its benefits in Volume 2 of my commercial newsletter, *Exploring the Creative Process of Market Research.* I search for the root causal problem and possible solutions to it from the beginning of a research project, as this approach is much more effective than searching for a solution after the research has been completed.

2. Horizontal versus Vertical Research

In my commercial work, whenever I was hired to conduct a big project, I first created what I call a "Research Bank." I would ask my client for his or her file including all the research done to date on the product or service I was to research further. I would then re-analyze each of the 25, 50, or 75 studies, and integrate the findings. Indeed, I wrote a research article on the Research Bank Technique, entitled "There's Gold in Them Thar' Research Files–the Research Bank," which was published in the journal *Marketing Review.* I call this approach "horizontal" research because many different research projects are studied in the course of the project, and I integrate the findings from all of them, as if they were a single project. This approach inevitably led me to a half dozen or more major new insights, which I would present to the client in a half-day or full-day presentation. This approach usually led me far along the road to the discovery of the root cause of the problem and often in the direction of a practical solution(s).

In contrast, what I call "vertical" research means one study at a time. In the article I wrote, I mention that after producing a Research Bank (horizontal research), I often got to know more about the original (vertical) study than the person who conducted that research, because I had learned so much else on the topic relating to the study. This is what happened in my research on the current subject.

An example: I had wondered why the middle class is eroding so quickly despite the fact that though its income is not increasing nearly as quickly as that of the rich, the median real household income increased from approximately $47,000 a year in 1980 to $55,000 a year in 2006 (DeNavas-Walkt, Proctor and Smith 2013). I found one answer to this question in a study by Elizabeth Warren (at the time of writing, a senator from Massachusetts) and her daughter, Amelia Warren Tyagi, which they describe in their excellent book, *The Two-Income Trap: Why Middle-Class Parents Are Going Broke* (Warren and Warren Tyagi 2003).

An explanation Warren and Tyagi offer is that despite a slightly higher household income, heavy costs are incurred when a second earner in the family enters the workplace. They compared a one-earner household in 1971 to a two-earner household in 2001 and found that the two families were left with a similar sum after fixed expenses. I get more specific on why in a later chapter.

I also learned another explanation to the same question on the erosion of the middle class from Bill Gross, CEO of Pimco until recently, by far the largest marketer of bonds in the world. Gross points out that in the 1990s, the way inflation is measured was changed. I get more specific about how in a later section, but for now let's just say that he believes that the US inflation rate is understated by at least 1% per year (Gross 2004).

Taking the two points into account over years, a worker's real wages (in terms of buying power) are significantly lower than reported.

3. Data-Driven Economics versus Orthodox Economics

In orthodox economics, there are many assumptions—or givens. Looking back, I think that a major reason much orthodox research has been less than successful in this area is that in the past three to four decades, the US has switched from a Business Economy to a *Stock Price Economy*, each with very different dynamics, while the orthodox economics has not changed accordingly to fit the new economic landscape.

Also, I believe that too many economists are slaves to what renowned economists dictated centuries ago, when the world was very different from what it is today. For example, the explanation I have seen most often for why any form of trade is positive for the US economy belongs to David Ricardo, an economist who lived 200 years ago. I believe that there are just too many assumptions and too many antiquated concepts accepted in today's economics—and that they simply don't work. This is not to say that I ignore what some smart economists said years ago. For example, I believe that Adam Smith's free market concept is still the most important idea in economics. However, even here, it is important that the free market be free.

For example, laissez faire (or deregulation) should not be seen as another term for the free market. Indeed, the existence of laissez faire without a free market is the source of many economic problems in the US—in fact, it is a major cause of the financial explosion that occurred in the early part of this century, which was followed by the Great Recession.

I call the approach I use "Data-Driven Economics" because it is built on data, with very few assumptions and essentially no mathematical models. I do use some concepts from orthodox economics, but only those that I believe are true and actually applicable today.

Part I

**Income Inequality and Poor Growth in
the New *Stock Price Economy***

CHAPTER 1
The Two Root Causes of Income Inequality

CHAPTER 2
**The Root Cause of the US Economy's Chronically
Poor Growth since the Great Recession**

CHAPTER 3
**Why Are Corporate Profits and Stock Prices
Soaring Despite a Weak Economy?**

The Two Root Causes
of Income Inequality

There has been much commentary, speculation, and even research on the cause(s) of Income Inequality in recent years.

This is because Income Inequality has escalated for more than 30 years as wealthy Americans (usually described as the top 1% in household income) have gained extraordinary economic success while the middle class and other ordinary Americans (often called "the 99%") suffer the effects of low wages, high unemployment, and high underemployment. Indeed, the large middle class for which the United States has long been renowned, is badly eroding—a process that is occurring faster and faster. From 1979 to 2007, the incomes of the top 1% increased from being 10 times those of median Americans to 29 times (Stone and Arloc 2010). In effect, Income Inequality had tripled. Also, in the three years after the Great Recession officially ended (June 2009), 95% of economic growth went to the wealthy (top 1% of income), leaving only 5% of economic growth to the other 99% of Americans (Federal Reserve Board 2014).

There has been a great deal of speculation about the cause(s) of Income Inequality, but I think that the explanations offered are essentially incorrect, incomplete, or both. A *New York Times* online questionnaire developed from economists and readers listed 14 possible reasons for low incomes (Leonhardt 2012). Personally, I ascribe to the old saying: "If you have ten reasons for something, you don't know the reason."

Two Commonly Suggested but Incorrect Sources
of Income Inequality

President Obama and others have suggested two perpetuators of Income Inequality (Obama 2013):

- A weak educational system
- Not enough innovation

But the president and the others are wrong.

A Weak Educational System

An improved educational system would help the US economically in the long run, but a poor educational system didn't cause Income Inequality—and improving the system will take a long time to achieve, and thus can't possibly affect Income Inequality until an unknown date far in the future.

The US unemployment rate was lower than most countries before the Great Recession began in 2007—yet higher than most other advanced countries (U.S. Division of International Labor Comparisons 2013) two years later (U.S. Bureau of Labor Statistics 2012) when the official recession ended. As educational quality in America couldn't have changed significantly in a two-year period, it doesn't appear to have had a direct effect on Income Inequality in the US.

Not Enough Innovation

President Obama and many others say that more innovation is necessary to solve the US Income Inequality problem. However, Andy Grove, who was CEO of Intel for 18 years, said (in an excellent article) that only 10% of the jobs in innovation are actually utilized in creating the innovation itself, while 90% of the jobs are in the scaling of the product engineering to learn how to manufacture the product and in manufacturing it, and the latter usually takes place in China. This results in high-tech companies like Apple and Dell employing only 10% of their workers in the US and 90% in China (Grove 2010).

Innovation, at least in electronics (where much of the innovation is today) as presently constituted, will more likely help solve the employment problem in China than it will in the US. According to Grove, the US needs to find a means to scale innovations here like it used to—and he offers a way, if controversial, to do it. Even Grove thinks that the US will be accused of a trade war if his approach is used, but thinks we should do what we do in wars: fight to win (Grove 2010).

My reaction is that we won't find solutions to the job problem unless we look thoroughly for them. Interestingly, Jeffrey Immelt, the CEO of GE, who the media has dubbed the "Job Czar," said that for such an important problem, there has been relatively little time and effort spent on the subject (Nisen 2013). Later in this book, I recommend that there be a separate Jobs Department, perhaps even at the Cabinet level.

The Two Root Causes

Rather than accepting the above reasons as sources of Income Inequality, I believe the problem can be attributed to the following:

1. The switch over time from a Business Economy to a *Stock Price Economy*
2. The loss of political power by the middle class and other ordinary Americans, which has led to the loss of workers' economic power

Let's examine each of these situations in detail.

The US Economy's Switch from a Business Economy to a Stock Price Economy

In the Business Economy, the CEO was interested in short-term profits, but he or she was also interested in medium- and long-term profits. The company was run to be successful for the long run. On the other hand, starting more than three decades ago, in the mid-to-late 1970s, the US began switching from a Business Economy to a *Stock Price Economy*. In the *Stock Price Economy*, the measure of success of a company or CEO is the change in the stock price, in particular during the short term—the previous three months and to some degree the estimate for the next three months, and the trend between the two (Mauboussin 2012). In the *Stock Price Economy*, even what's considered long-term—the rest of the financial year—is short, only 12 months or less.

In the *Stock Price Economy*, the stock price is the criterion of success for both the company and the CEO. CEOs and top management often receive stock options based on the success (or lack of success) of the stock price—the higher the stock price, the higher the value of these stock options. This results in higher compensation for the CEO and top management, as these stock options often comprise the majority of their compensation, especially for the CEO.

There is much talk about companies making too many decisions based on short-term value—and that this is bad for business. While this brand of thinking is often a good idea for the company stock price and for the compensation of the CEO and top management, it can be a bad idea for the medium- and long-term success of the company, as well as for the workers and the overall US economy.

Following is a quote from Stephen A. Schwarzman, the co-founder of Blackstone, who currently heads the massive private equity company. He made it clear to *Businessweek* (in 1996) that CEOs are "...not able to do some of the things they know should be done to fix their companies. If it requires their (corporate) earnings to be deferred for two or three quarters (not even a full year) or to make write-offs, they'd rather not do the right thing because if they do, they'll be penalized by their stockholders." (Sorkin 2013)

This penalization he refers to denotes a decrease in stock price, and thus a lower compensation.

Increasing Short-Term Profits and Stock Prices by Lowering Labor Costs

CEOs and top management have learned that the easiest and surest way to increase short-term corporate profits, and thus the stock price, is to lower costs—and the simplest and most dependable way to lower expenses is to lower labor costs. "Stockholder value," a term frequently used, is often little more than the increasing or decreasing of the short-term stock price. CEOs ask themselves whether an action will increase the short-term stock price—not whether the action will actually improve (or truly grow) the business.

Not only do labor costs account for much of the cost of producing the average product or service, but the percentage of private sector employees who have negotiating power with management regarding wages, benefits, pensions, etc. has fallen by 80% since the 1950s to under 7% (from a high of 35%) (Hirsch 2011). Also, because top management has seen the union movement collapse, and is no longer afraid that non-union workers will join or form a union, it has unilaterally ended the unwritten contract to treat non-union workers well. Therefore, the CEO can most often control labor costs.

Certainly, lowering labor costs is a surer way to increase short-term corporate profits—and thus the stock price—than a strategy of building new products. New products take a long time to develop, which can hurt profits until completed—not to mention the fact that many new products fail. In the *Stock Price Economy*, lowering labor costs has allowed US companies to increase profits and stock prices, even in a very weak economy (Hall 2011). Recently, I read a quote from a CEO to the effect that his company had learned how to make money in an economy that rose by a mere 1% of GDP per year. This is why corporate profits and stock prices have managed to soar since the Great Recession ended, despite a fragile economy in which the middle class has eroded.

In a major sense, American business is being penny-wise and pound foolish. Cutting down on wages and jobs is reducing the ability of consumers to buy what the company sells. It is "starving" its customers. Also, the consumer economy accounts for more than two-thirds of the total US economy (Reuters 2016).

Here are some of the ways CEOs and top management cut labor costs:

1. **Outsourcing to low-wage countries**, often to manufacture the item and then bring it back to the US to market it (Lach 2012).

2. **Keeping wages down**—not too difficult to accomplish with a small, weak labor movement in the private sector. More than 9 out of 10 workers (93%) in the private sector have no person or institution to represent them in negotiations for wages, benefits, pensions, etc. with top management (U.S. Bureau of Labor Statistics 2016).

3. **Reducing the labor force and keeping it down.** During the recent Great Recession, American CEOs and top management laid off a far higher percentage of workers than other advanced economies—and have kept their workforces down for a long time—which has led to long-term chronic unemployment and underemployment (those with temporary jobs, part-time jobs, or private contractor jobs but who would prefer a full-time job) (U.S. Bureau of Labor Statistics 2012).

4. **Increasing the number of contingent workers**—workers who want a full-time job but can only get temporary, part-time, or independent contractor work. Contingent jobs tend to be low paying and have few or no benefits—and they are even easier to let go than full-time employees (U.S. Government Accountability Office 2015). They might be called "throwaway workers" (Morris and Mitchell 2012).

5. **Sharply lowering the percentage of workers with defined-benefit pensions** (paid for by the company) and sharply increasing the percentage of workers with defined contribution pensions, including 401Ks (most or all of which is generally paid for by the workers themselves) (U.S. Employee Benefits Security Administration 1999).

6. **Ending the cost-of-living adjustment**. This approach used to be very popular. Unions in the private sector, which in the main are very weak today, no longer even ask that the contract include a cost-of-living benefit.

7. **Taking advantage of unpaid internships**. In recent years, many companies capitalize on this opportunity to give college students "experience" for little or no pay (Burger 2014).

Here are some other ways that Americans treat workers worse than other advanced economies and some not-so-advanced countries:

1. The US is the only advanced economy in the world that does not offer a minimum number of paid vacation days by law. Workers in the other advanced countries take from two to three times as many paid vacation days as American workers, while one in four American workers receives no paid vacation days at all (Johnston 2014).

2. Nearly all of the other countries with advanced economies guarantee workers a minimum number of paid sick days by law. In the US, on the other hand, 40% of American workers get no minimum days of paid sick leave at all (Ingraham 2015).

3. Nearly all advanced countries offer a minimum of paid maternal/paternal leave by law—but not the US (Kurtzleben 2015).

4. The US is the only country with an advanced economy that doesn't have

universal healthcare (Fisher 2012). Even if ObamaCare is a successful healthcare system, there still will be millions of Americans without healthcare insurance (Barry-Jester and Casselman 2015). Elsewhere, healthcare insurance is seen as a right—but not in the US (Book 2013). I consider failing to offer someone healthcare insurance a cruel and unusual punishment. It is cruel because research estimates that 45,000 Americans die each year because they don't have healthcare insurance (Robertson 2009). There is also little doubt that millions of Americans put off medical care because of cost, and worsen their health issue because of it. It is unusual because the US is the only country with an advanced economy that doesn't have universal healthcare.

Although the government votes these benefits in, the company must pay for them. It is no wonder that companies lobby against laws that will cost them money. But wouldn't the lives of Americans be greatly improved with a guaranteed minimum number of days of paid vacation leave, paid sick leave, paid parental leave, and even guaranteed healthcare? Absolutely yes.

It was considered a big deal in the US when Bill Clinton passed a bill that allowed Americans to take some unpaid personal leave. It certainly isn't a big deal compared with what people receive in other countries with advanced economies.

A Worsening Situation for Many Workers

The problem is that a new approach being used by companies to lower labor costs can cause major complications for the worker's family. The *New York Times* article "Working Anything but 9 to 5" discusses the approach and its effects in a first-page story published on August 13, 2014 (Kantor 2014). The following quotes come directly from the article:

- "Along with virtually every retail and restaurant chain, Starbucks relies on software that choreographs workers in precise, intricate ballets, using sales patterns and other data to determine which of its 130,000 baristas are needed in its thousands of locations and exactly when. Big box retailers or mall clothing chains are now capable of bringing in more hands in anticipation of a delivery truck pulling in or the weather changing, and sending workers home when real-time analyses show sales are slowing. Managers are often compensated based on the efficiency of their staffing."

- "Scheduling is now a powerful tool to bolster profits, allowing businesses to cut labor costs with a few keystrokes. 'It's like magic,' said Charles DeWitt, vice president for business development at Kronos, which supplies the software for Starbucks and many other chains."

- "'Yet those advances are injecting turbulence into parents' routines and personal relationships, undermining efforts to expand preschool access, driving some mothers out of the work force and redistributing some of the uncertainty of doing business from corporations to families,' say parents, child-care providers, and policy experts."

Here are some examples:
- "In Brooklyn, Sandianna Irvine often works "on call" hours at Ashley Stewart, a plus-size clothing store, rushing to make arrangements for her five-year-old daughter if the store needs her."
- "Before Martha Cadenas was promoted to manager at a Walmart in Apple Valley, Minn., she had to work any time the store needed; her mother 'ended up having to move in with me,' she said, because of the unpredictable hours."
- "Maria Trisler is often dismissed early from her shifts at McDonald's in Peoria, Ill., when the computers say sales are slow."
- "The same sometimes happens to Ms. Navarro (the central person whose situation is discussed in the article) at Starbucks."
- "Saturday afternoon of the Fourth of July weekend, Ms. Navarro has made it through 'clopening,' closing late at night and opening again just a few hours later. But she has not yet worked up the courage to ask Ms. Rivera (a close friend of Rivera's boyfriend, Oscar Nunez) for help the next day with Gavin (Ms. Rivera's five-year-old)."
- Finally, there is the blurb used by the reporters to describe the pictures used in the article to depict Ms. Nunez' trip to work: "Janette Navarro,

working at a Starbucks in San Diego, where she rarely learned her schedule more than three days before the start of a workweek. Nick Martinez, Ms. Navarro's boyfriend at the time, helped her and her son, Gavin, prepare for the day. Mr. Martinez served as the surrogate father to Gavin. Ms. Navarro and Gavin, below, headed off for a day that started with a three-hour commute." (Mr. Martinez eventually left Ms. Navarro—one factor being the chaos of the job.)

The software not only increases profits but wreaks havoc on the workers and his or her family. There are millions of American workers who feel helpless on the job and have no representation in the negotiation process.

There is a dynamic that speaks to the difference between the economic recovery in the 1980s and the current recovery. In the recovery of the 1980s, it became clear that much of the problem in the US was due to the poor quality of its products. As a result, a strong drive began to improve quality, including prizes given for success in doing so. This improvement in quality was very helpful in improving the American economy.

In today's "recovery," on the other hand, there is no such drive for quality improvement. It is almost as if some US companies have given up on manufacturing products in America. It may even be that Apple (and the other large electronic companies) is more interested in improving quality in China than here in the US, because Apple's (and the other large electronic companies) products are manufactured in China (Langlois 2015).

Siphoning off Workers' Wages to Increase Corporate Profits (and Thus the Stock Price)

In the three decades after World War II, real worker wages increased by 91% of labor productivity. This is the way it has been for many years, with workers getting the very large percentage of increased labor productivity. However, in the three recent decades between 1979 to 2013, real worker wages have increased by only 8% compared to an increase of 64.9% in productivity. Real wages increased by only 12% of productivity (Gould 2014).

This is based on the report *The Sad Story of Wages in America* by Lawrence Mishel and Heidi Shierholz (Shierholz and Mishel 2011). Workers across the board—whether in the private or public sector, high-school- or college-educated—have suffered decades of wage stagnation despite large gains in productivity.

The decrease in the percentage of wages labor got from productivity between the three decades after World War II and the three decades from 1979 to 2009 is 78% of productivity (from 91% to 13%) (Bivens, et al. 2014). If workers in the three decades between 1979 to 2009 continued to receive 91% of productivity—if management didn't siphon off 78% of the productivity that used to go to labor, workers would have received raises totaling about $36,600 a year (78% of $47,000) in 2009.

Without the siphoning, the median household would have received a wage increase from $47,000 to $83,600 a year. This would have solved or at least greatly reduced the Income Inequality problem of the American people as well as the "demand" problem of the US economy. Today, many American workers do not earn enough from their jobs to fulfill their needs, which negatively affects both themselves and the overall economy. On the other hand, it is this siphoning of what used to be paid to workers that is the main reason for the great increase in corporate profits and stock prices. And, because the wealthy (top 1%) dominate ownership of stocks and bonds, this also explains much of Income Inequality, with the income of the top 1% soaring (Bivens, et al. 2014). There is no question that there would be some increase in product and service prices, but solvent Americans could easily afford to pay a little more for goods and services.

Income Inequality grew quickly after the Great Recession officially ended. In the first three years since it officially ended, the top 1% received 95% of the increase in US growth, leaving 5% for the other 99% of Americans (Saez 2013). If we consider the top 5%, they received 107% of US economic growth, meaning that the bulk of Americans actually had a decrease in growth. Many millions of Americans were still in recession.

$20 an Hour for Denmark's Fast-Food Workers

"A number of American fast-food workers are fighting for what many consider an outlandish minimum wage—$15 an hour. Employers say this is impossible. Yet, an October 27, 2014 *New York Times* article entitled "Living Wages, Rarity for US Fast-Food Workers, Served up in Denmark" describes the case of Hampus Elofsson with his 40-hour-a-week job at a Danish Burger King at $20 an hour (Alderman and Greenhouse 2014). As Mr. Elofsson says, "You can make a decent living here by working in fast food. You don't have to struggle to get by." A burger costs $5.40 in Denmark compared to $4.80 in the US.

The question is why US fast-food employers can't pay the $15 an hour workers are clamoring for if Danish fast-food employers can make a profit (though not as big) while paying workers $20 an hour?

In Denmark, fast-food workers are guaranteed benefits that their American counterparts could only dream of. Under the industry's collective agreement, there are five weeks' paid vacation, paid maternity and paternity leave, and a pension plan. Workers must be paid overtime for working after 6 P.M., and on Sundays.

Unlike most American fast-food workers, the Danes often get their work schedules four weeks in advance, and employees cannot be sent home early without pay just because business slows.

The Dilemma of Middle-Class Families Living Paycheck to Paycheck

Why has the middle class eroded so quickly over the past three decades? After all, the median US household has increased its annual income from $47,000 to $55,000 from 1980 to 2006 (DeNavas-Walkt, Proctor and Smith 2013). It appears that there are in fact two main causes.

1. High fixed costs of the second earner entering the workplace.
Massachusetts Senator and former Harvard Professor Elizabeth Warren, along with her daughter, Amelia Warren Tyagi, have researched this issue and published the results in their book, *The Two-Income*

Trap: Why Middle-Class Parents Are Going Broke (Warren and Warren Tyagi 2003). They found that there are considerable fixed costs that accompany a second earner going to work. The second earner has to pay income tax, often placing the family in a higher tax bracket, as well as Social Security and Medicare payroll taxes. He or she must also buy and maintain a second automobile, provide childcare or preschool care, pay more for housing, especially if it is near a good school, and pay more for the high inflation costs for healthcare and higher education, etc.

2. **An understatement of inflation.** During the last 30 years, the way inflation was measured changed in a way that lowered the inflation rate (Cornerstone Wealth Management, LLC 2011):

   - For example, if a cut of meat increased significantly in price, it was taken for granted that the consumer would buy a cheaper cut of meat.
   - Also, those measuring inflation now easily accepted improvements in quality in a way that significantly increased the worth of the product or service—often more than they should have. For example, if a new computer is 15% faster than the previous one, those computing the inflation rate might assume that the new computer was 15% superior—even if the speed of the computer at that level did not really improve its overall performance that much.
   - Housing equations, which account for 42% of costs in the inflation computation, also changed. It used to simply be the average price of a house that was used. Now, it is more complex. It is based on how much the house is worth in rental terms. At the time of the change, home prices were rising at three times the new criterion of housing.

Bill Gross, who was CEO (until recently) of the largest bond fund company in the US (perhaps in the world) and who is known as the "king of bonds," believes that the inflation rate is at least 1% per year higher than announced (Gross 2004). This would mean that the GDP and real wages of the US are 1% lower per year than announced, because both measurements use the inflation rate as the base. It would also mean that in the 20 years since the inflation rate has changed, the after-inflation income of the US would be significantly lower than the one that was announced.

The heavy fixed extra costs of the second earner entering the marketplace combined with the substantial reduction of the true inflation rate sharply reduces the real spending power of the family. It radically reduces the real buying power of Americans and helps explain why the middle class has eroded so badly, even though household income data have not fallen out of bed. It helps explain why the increase in so many families from a single earner to two earners has not resulted in the growth of the middle class.

Unless we end the *Stock Price Economy*, even a so-called improved US economy won't stop the erosion of the American middle class. Technically speaking, the US has seen some good economic times in the past 30 years, but middle-class erosion continues.

Keeping Profits High by Increasing Unemployment

During the recent Great Recession, US companies discovered that an excellent way to substantially increase profits even more was to sharply reduce their workforces. Even after the recession officially ended, these companies have kept their workforces as small as possible, keeping unemployment rates as high as possible.

Table 1 ranks 10 countries from 1 to 10 on the change in the unemployment rate from January 2007 to January 2010 (essentially the periods before and after the Great Recession). The change between the two years is in the right column, and in the two columns to the left of it are the unemployment rates in January 2007 and January 2010 (U.S. Bureau of Labor Statistics 2012).

Some key findings from Table 1:

- During the Great Recession, the employment rate of the US fell (or was pushed) much more than the country with the next highest increase of the unemployment rate, England (5.1% to 3.6%)—or 1.5% more than England.
- If the US unemployment rate during the Great Recession had risen as much as the next highest country (England), the US would have had an unemployment rate in 2010, post-recession, of only 8.2% (9.7% minus 1.5%).
- If the US unemployment rate had risen as much as the next highest country (England), the US would have lost about 1.5 million fewer jobs than it did (1.5% of 100+ million jobs)

Table 1

Ranked Increase in Unemployment Rate for
10 Industrial Countries from 2007 2010

Rank	Country	Unemployment Rate, January 2007	Unemployment Rate, January 2010	Change
1	United States	4.6%	9.7%	+5.1%
2	United Kingdom	5.6%	8.0%	+3.6%
3	Sweden	6.5%	8.7%	+2.2%
4	Italy	6.3%	8.4%	+2.1%
5	Canada	5.4%	7.4%	+2.0%
6.5	Japan	3.8%	4.8%	+1.0%
6.5	France	8.7%	9.7%	+1.0%
8	Australia	4.5%	5.3%	+0.8%
9	Netherlands	4.0%	4.6%	+0.6%
10	Germany	9.3%	7.6%	(-1.7%)

(The average increase in unemployment of the nine countries other than the US was +1.3 %)

Note that the countries other than the US lost an average of 1.3% of their workers during the Great Recession, compared to 5.1% in the US. Some of Germany's great results in unemployment are partially due to its "share the work" program. Instead of being laid off, workers in the program worked three days a week. And the government used its bully pulpit to get companies signed onto the program (Center for Economic and Policy Research 2012).

Also, the companies had something to gain. When the economy did turn around, German companies could quickly increase production. This is especially important in Germany, which is strong in advanced engineering and needs experienced engineers and others to produce products.

More recently, the US economy has done better than some of the other advanced countries. I believe this is due to the US having much money thrown into the economy by the Federal Reserve Bank while most of the other countries with advanced economies used austerity budgets, which kept growth in abeyance. These countries did not throw money into the economy because they were afraid of inflation, which hasn't happened in the US. Some of them are starting to rethink their situation. The Republicans are still pushing for an austerity budget that would take money out of the economy.

American Companies Wield Far More Power over Their Employees

The American Heritage Foundation, a conservative think tank, annually presents what it calls "Economic Freedom" ratings (100 is the highest rating; 1 is the lowest). There is an overall rating developed from the average of 10 separate ratings, one of which is labor freedom (all ratings are from the frame of reference of the employer).

Table 2 ranks seven countries on their labor freedom rating (from the frame of reference of employers). We also computed the labor freedom ratings of the countries from the frame of reference of workers by subtracting the employer freedom rating from 100. The US has a labor freedom rating of 91 from the frame of reference of the employer, so it has a labor freedom rating of only 9 from the frame of reference of the worker.

As can be seen in Table 2, US employers have far more freedom with their workers than do those in the other six countries (American Heritage Foundation 2016). The US receives a near-perfect rating of 91, far higher than the second highest country, China, which has a rating of 62. Germany receives a freedom with workers rating (from the frame of reference of the employer) of only 51, a bit more than half that of the US. American employers have far more freedom with workers than do German employers. On the other hand, Germany and the other countries have a much higher rating of labor rights than the US. For example, from the worker frame of reference, Germany has a labor rating that is more than five times as high as the US (49% to 9%).

Table 2

Labor Freedom Ratings from the Frame of Reference
of Employers and Employees of Seven Countries

Country	Labor Freedom Rating (From Employer Point of View)	Labor Freedom Rating (From Employee Point of View)
United States	91%	9%
China	62%	38%
Brazil	53%	48%
Germany	51%	49%
India	48%	57%
South Korea	47%	53%
France	43%	57%
(Average of six countries other than the US)	51%	49%

Must American Companies Treat Their Workers so Shabbily?

The short answer is "no." There is an irony in Americans being refused social programs and important parts of a safety net because, we are told, it would otherwise hurt the US's competitive position in the global economy. General Electric CEO Jeffrey Immelt, appointed head of a committee on how the US can increase exports, concluded that the US is not trying hard enough to win business overseas. "We haven't really tried as hard as we can to compete, educate and sell our products around the world, and I think we can do better." (Malone 2011)

Immelt offered Germany as an example of a wealthy country that has been successful in pushing exports: "Chancellor (Angela) Merkel flies from Berlin to Beijing, there's 25 German CEOs that go on the plane right behind her. And they connect the dots. They play hard, they play to win."

Corporate claims in the US that cutting wages and other "costs" are a necessity for competing effectively in the global economy seems to be an excuse rather than an explanation.

Germany treats its workers much better than American companies or the American government do. According to American conventional wisdom, Germany must have a major problem competing in the global economy. This is not the case. Germany is in the world's top two countries in trade surpluses, and exports twice as much to the US as it imports. On the other hand, America has by far the largest trade deficit in the world. In a major sense, Germany seems more proficient in the ways of capitalism than the US.

My explanation for the above is cynical. I think that American companies treat their workers shabbily to save money—not because they wish to be more competitive in the global economy. I think they treat their workers poorly because they want to make as much corporate profit as possible while raising their stock price as high as possible—workers be damned.

Let's give a couple of examples that prove that the above paragraph is not just theoretical. Caterpillar, a giant, very profitable company, recently instituted a two-tier wage system. Longer-term workers were forced to accept a six-year wage freeze and newer workers had to be satisfied with a significantly lower wage. That was okay with CEO Douglas Oberhelman. Yet Mr. Oberhelman's compensation increased by more than 80% in the last two years. Oberhelman is quoted to have said: "We can never make enough profit," (Nisen 2013), while a Seattle entrepreneur was quoted saying, "Employers pay their work forces as much as they are forced to and no more. There's no compelling reason to give raises." (Greenhouse 2013)

These two quotes show the vulnerability of American workers in the private sector. Not all CEOs are so harsh, but one must realize that CEOs and top management are financially motivated to lower labor costs. This approach leads to higher corporate profits, a higher stock price, and eventually to higher compensation for the CEO and top management. It is an unfortunate—and unfair—place for American workers to be, and is the case largely because they have nobody and no institution to represent them in negotiations with management on wages, benefits, pensions, etc.

All, or nearly all, the power is on the side of the employer. If workers are to have any chance of stopping and turning around Income Inequality, they need more power. A separate section of the report recommends an institution that can help the middle class and other ordinary people get political power, and thus economic power—which brings us to the second root cause of the Income Inequality problem.

A Lack of Workers' Political Power, Leading to an Absence of Economic Power

I have already hinted at the second root causal problem of Income Inequality. Despite the fact that 47% of Americans see themselves as middle class (Pew Research Center 2015), and an estimated 10% aspire to the middle class (my estimate)—about 60% in all, in actuality the middle class has very little political power, which results in very little economic power.

What a difference from the past. For example, Franklin Roosevelt exulted in calling his enemies "the economic royalists" (Roosevelt 1936). Today, both political parties have shifted significantly to the right. The Democratic Party is admittedly pro-business—at least that's what they tell Wall Street and big companies when they ask for large campaign contributions. The Democratic Party no longer represents just the middle class and other ordinary Americans, and it's sometimes hard to tell the difference between certain Democrats and Republicans.

It doesn't seem to matter that the base of the Democratic Party is liberal. The leadership tends to be centrist, while the Republicans have moved sharply to the Right Wing. Bill Clinton called his approach the "third way"; he was a triangulator. Clinton took some of his thinking from the Left and some from the Right. And Obama, despite his liberal words, headed in an essentially similar direction. As a result, the middle class and other ordinary Americans have suffered through more than 30 years of Income Inequality. And despite the lack of representation of workers in the private sector, there seems to be little or no mention of labor union reform, despite the fact that both the workers and the overall economy were strong when unions were strong.

Later, you will find a chapter devoted to why it is both critical and difficult for workers to make the union movement stronger. Very simply, when unions were stronger, workers fared much better economically; since they have collapsed, the middle class is also collapsing. We will also explore how middle-class reform can come to pass.

Also, although the American people coped better economically in the Bill Clinton administration than in the Ronald Reagan and George W. Bush administrations, the 1% increased their incomes four times as much as the 99% did during the Clinton administration. Also, Wall Street was deregulated mainly during the Clinton administration. This led to the financial disaster of 2008 and then to the Great Recession.

In my opinion, the only way the middle class can reclaim its power—both political and economic—is to develop an organization to take it back. A later section of this book details how I see such an organization.

The Current State of Income Inequality

The most commonly used measure of Income Inequality is the Gini Coefficient. Below, Table 3 shows this Income Inequality measure in the US from 1967 to 2007 (Oak 2012):

Table 3
The Gini Coefficient from 1967 to 2007

Year 1967	2007	Change
Gini Coefficient 39.7	46.9	+18.1%

The Problems with the Gini Coefficient Measure

Three major weaknesses of the Gini Coefficient measure can be seen in Table 3:

- It is a mathematical concept, which doesn't make sense to most people, as they don't naturally think in this way. People tend to think arithmetically (linearly) rather than mathematically. This will be explained later in this chapter.
- The Gini Coefficient makes Income Inequality seem much lower than it really is. I think this could be one reason why people are not as upset

about the issue of Income Inequality as one might expect them to be.

- The Gini Coefficient shows little variation during what is actually a time of great variation in Income Inequality. Over the last four decades, during which Income Inequality has massively increased (seen in Table 4), the Gini Coefficient increased by only 18.1%. This is misleading and makes the problem seem much less important to politicians and voters than it really is.

The New Income Inequality Ratio

As a result of the weaknesses in the Gini Coefficient, I developed a measure of Income Inequality that I believe deals effectively with its problems. This new Inequality Index is calculated by dividing the annual household income of the top 1% of income by the household income of the median household. The new measure is useful because it is easy to understand (i.e., more in line with the way people think) and is much more sensitive to variation in Income Inequality than the Gini Coefficient.

Table 4 shows the Income Inequality Ratio every five years from 1980 to 2006:

Table 4
Top 1%, Median Household Income,
and the Income Inequality Ratio

Year	Top 1%	Middle Quintile (Median)	Income Inequality Ratio
1980	$488,200	$49,300	10 to 1
1985	$654,400	$49,600	13 to 1
1990	$774,500	$51,600	15 to 1
1995	$864,400	$53,200	16 to 1
2000	$1,460,600	$57,000	26 to 1
2005	$1,558,500	$58,500	27 to 1
2006	$1,743,700	$60,700	29 to 1

The Income Inequality Index Has Tripled in 26 years

Using the new approach, the Income Inequality Ratio is shown to have increased from 10 to 1 in 1980, to 29 to 1 in 2006—essentially tripling in 26 years. In other words, the average household in the top 1% of incomes tripled its income relative to the median income household. I think it will be easier for economists and the American people to understand this new measure of Income Inequality, and they will be more likely to realize how much of a problem this is.

This approach is arithmetic (linear) because the difference is tripled. The Gini Coefficient follows mathematical logic. In a 40-year period, the increase in the Gini Coefficient was only 18.1%.

What is most shocking (at least to me), is that within this 25-year period, the top 1% in household income have increased their real income (after inflation) from $488,200 to $1,538,500 a year—or by 218%.

What Is Happening to Income Inequality Today?

Five years after the Great Recession ended, how is Income Inequality doing? Not well. Table 5 compares the wages of jobs lost in the recession to the wages of jobs gained in the recovery (NELP 2014):

Table 5
Wages of Jobs Lost in the Recession versus
Those Gained in the Recovery

	Jobs Lost in the Recession	Jobs Gained in the Recovery
Higher-Wage Occupations ($21.14 to $54.55)	41%	30%
Mid-Wage Occupations ($13.84 to $21.13)	37%	26%
Lower-Wage Occupations ($7.69 to $13.83)	22%	44%
	100%	100%

The data in Table 5 show that:

- The percentage of higher-wage jobs lost and gained before (41%) and after (30%) the recession showed that the amount of higher-wage jobs decreased by 37%.
- The percentage of mid-wage jobs lost and gained before (37%) and after (26%) the recession show that the amount of mid-wage jobs decreased by 42%.
- The percentage of jobs in lower-wage occupations increased from 22% lost in the recession to 44% of jobs gained in the recovery.
- Basically, the jobs lost during the Great Recession were predominantly higher-wage and mid-wage jobs, while jobs gained in the recovery were predominantly lower-wage jobs. This substantially increases the Income Inequality and doesn't augur well for the future

Recently, the Dow Jones Index has about doubled since the Great Recession (MacroTrends 2016), while real wages have stalled, or even decreased. Income Inequality in the US seems to be gaining speed. This helps explain why in the past few years companies are doing so well in corporate profits and stock prices, while the middle class is falling apart.

Chapter 2

The Root Cause of the US Economy's Chronically Poor Growth since the Great Recession

The Root Cause of Slow Economic Growth

The reasons for the slow growth of our current economy in its attempt at recovery are generally different from the root causes of Income Inequality—most of the reasons relate more directly to actions taken by companies themselves and less to workers. The specifics are discussed later in this section.

The economy has come out of the Great Recession looking more like a lamb than a lion. Even though Americans built up their needs for products and services, economic growth has been very slow and faltering, averaging 1.4% per year during the six years after the recession (The World Bank 2016). Why is this?

Factors behind the Overall Weak Economy since the Great Recession

Some say that economies fare poorly after recessions caused by a major financial problem. However, there are specific causes that appear to be more related to the weak recovery from the recent recession.

1. Companies Keeping Labor Costs Down and "Starving" Customers

By keeping labor costs down (keeping wages down and unemployment and underemployment up), companies have pushed short-term corporate profits up—but at the expense of customers (Lazonick 2014). Some say we have a "supply-side" economy, but David Stockman, President Ronald Reagan's first Budget Director and lead man on the first Reagan tax cut, admitted in an interview in *The Atlantic* magazine that "supply-side" is really just the old Republican "trickle-down" economics, but that "trickle-down" philosophy is difficult to sell to the people (Greider 1981). I believe that we really have a demand-side economy, meaning that things only start rolling when consumers start buying. When consumers buy, companies work hard to produce the products and services that are being purchased, or are in demand. It is important to remember that consumer buying accounts for close to 70% of the GDP (The World Bank 2015). Ironically, by keeping wages down and unemployment and underemployment up, many companies are "starving" their would-be customers.

Also, the low wages, high unemployment, and high underemployment result in less revenue for the government (e.g., in taxes), and cause the government to spend a great deal of money on unemployment insurance, food stamps, etc.—not to mention raising issues with the budget deficit.

2. Companies Reducing Spending to Buy Back Their Own Stock

In the *Stock Price Economy*, many companies cut down on spending to grow the company in order to buy back their own stock. Some companies even go so far as to borrow money to do this. Buying back stock is an artificial way to increase the stock price by dividing the same amount of profit by a lower number of stock shares available, but reducing the amount of money reinvested in the company will often hurt the company in the medium and long term. However, the higher stock price makes the company and the CEO look good, because the stock price increases and the CEO's stock options therefore increase in value.

Buying back stock in the company, however, does nothing for the company. I've read it described as taking money from the left pocket and putting it in the right pocket—but it's most often successful in artificially increasing the stock price.

3. Companies Cutting Down on Investment in the Company

In the *Stock Price Economy*, when a company makes a big investment in the business, the stock price often goes down. I remember reading an interview with the CEO of a giant hotel chain. He said that he wanted to refurbish the entire hotel chain, but that "you can't do that in a public company." This is because spending a lot of money to keep the company successful long term is likely to lower short-term profits, so the stock price would probably decrease. This is a similar point to that made by Stephen Schwarzman, co-founder of the private equity firm Blackstone, in the previous chapter. (In the *Stock Price Economy*), Schwarzman said that the CEO will not do what he knows would fix the company if he or she will be punished by a lower stock price (even if only for two or three quarters—less than a year) (Sorkin 2013).

4. Switching to the Stock Price Economy, Leading to Short-Term Thinking and Behavior

Many say that there is too much short-term thinking in American business. The reason for this is not because CEOs think this is best for their companies. Rather, short-term thinking is best for the stock price in our current *Stock Price Economy*. Consider that the average CEO is only going to hold his post for a limited amount of time, and many CEOs want to make their "pile" during their years as CEO. Similarly, a private equity company is usually going to keep a company for only a few years, and its financial return is their main concern. Too often, the private equity company will even put a company at risk by borrowing a great deal of money, often in an effort to declare a large special dividend to itself.

I remember reading an article about an otherwise profitable company (Simmons Co, maker of the well-known Beautyrest mattress) that had to go into bankruptcy because seven different private equity companies had owned it for a time and several of them had allotted to themselves sizable special dividends (Reuters 2009).

5. When Companies Are More Powerful than Government

I think that a major problem with the US economy is that companies seem to have more power than the government. I remember reading about a conversation between President Obama and Steve Jobs, the genius CEO of Apple. Obama was asking Jobs about all the jobs Apple was outsourcing to China. Jobs replied something to the effect that those jobs were not coming back (Tau 2012). My reaction was: "I thought I voted for Obama for president, not Jobs." Why doesn't Obama push laws that motivate companies to keep work and workers in the US, like he said he would when he ran for president?

Compare this with the situation in Germany at the beginning of the Great Recession. The government realized that production would go down, and fewer workers would be needed. As mentioned earlier, it started a "share the work" program which, rather than laying workers off, had each worker work three days a week. The Great Recession caused far less unemployment in Germany than in the US. Also, German companies were more prepared to go full speed ahead when the economy turned around.

However, it wasn't all good for Germany. Productivity (measured as output divided by the number of workers used to produce that output) went way down because they kept so many workers, while in the US, productivity actually increased during the Great Recession because they let so many workers go. The main point here is that Germany was willing to suffer a major decrease in productivity in order to keep its workers working. The US was not. Indeed, American CEOs saw the Great Recession as an excellent opportunity to further cut labor costs and in so doing increase corporate profits and the stock price (Lazonick 2014).

Interestingly, some German multinationals helped the German employment situation by first letting go of its employees overseas. In a later section, we compare "flag-waving" patriotism with "economic" patriotism, both of which many German companies seem to possess. Many US companies, on the other hand, do not seem to have much "economic" patriotism. American CEOs tend not to put their money ("economic" patriotism) where their mouth is ("flag-waving" patriotism).

6. Less Antagonism between Employers and Employees in Germany

One major difference between the relationship of management to workers in the US and Germany is that you don't see as much antagonism between the two in Germany as you do in the US. Indeed, there is a law in Germany that an employee must be included on the board of directors of a large company. Workers know that the company must be successful in order for them to do well economically, but, unlike the case very often in the US, the German workers succeed if the German company succeeds.

Indeed, German companies usually have works councils where representatives of workers meet, sometimes to discuss how the company can be improved. Again, workers know that in order for them to do well (including keeping their jobs), the company must be performing well financially.

I also remember reading an interview of a German CEO of a large multinational company (I think it was Siemens). The CEO shocked the interviewer by saying that he would never make a big move regarding the company without talking to the union first.

Take the case of how a Volkswagen (German automobile company) factory in Tennessee handled a vote on establishing a works council. The company was neutral as far as the vote was concerned, but a US senator and the governor of the state interceded to warn the workers that if they passed the works council vote, the company would not expand at that site (Resnikoff 2014). Not surprisingly, the works council idea didn't come to fruition. Actually, the actions on the part of at least the senator were probably illegal. This example demonstrates how difficult it is to develop a representative body for workers in the US—especially in the South, but also in the country as a whole. (Interestingly, Volkswagen went ahead and treated the branch and its workers as if the workers had voted yes even though they voted no.)

7. Zero-Sum Profit-Thinking Versus True-Growth Thinking

In a major sense, many US companies see corporate profits in a zero-sum manner. The more they save on labor and capital costs, the higher the short-term positive effect on corporate profits and stock prices. CEOs love this approach because there is little short-term risk involved.

In a Business Economy, there is risk. CEOs must spend money for labor and capital goods they think will develop product growth (sales) in the future. The approach most often taken in the new *Stock Price Economy* augurs poorly for the future of the US economy. By definition, only being concerned about the short term leads not only to short-term thinking but limits true growth of the company, and eventually true growth of the US economy.

Chapter 3

Why Are Corporate Profits and Stock Prices Soaring Despite a Weak Economy?

One often hears that soaring corporate profits and stock prices are a positive reflection of the US economy. This used to be the case in the Business Economy, when stock prices most often reflected the actual state of the economy. However, in the *Stock Price Economy*, corporate profits and stock prices are soaring only because the companies are decreasing labor and capital costs. The result is that workers are too often hurting, and so is the economy as a whole. CEOs realize that lower labor and capital goods costs lead to higher short-term corporate profits and stock prices, but these damage both workers and the overall economy.

How a Corporate Focus on Short-Term Benefits Can Prove Harmful

US Companies Prospering at the Expense of American Labor

CEOs have learned that the surest way to increase short-term corporate profits, and thus the short-term stock price, is to reduce costs. Earlier, we named and discussed many of the major techniques companies have used, and continue to use, to cut labor costs. Recently, American CEOs have found another way to increase corporate profits and thus the stock price.

Because labor accounts for much of the total cost of producing a product or service, it makes the most sense to the CEO to concentrate on cutting labor costs. The US used to have a relatively low unemployment rate, but it reduced its workforce more quickly than other advanced countries during the Great Recession, and tried to keep the workforce at a relatively low level for a longer time than is usual after a recession.

US Companies Profiting to the Ill Effect
of the American Economy

Companies have kept costs down in a number of ways that have led to higher short-term corporate profits and higher stock prices but have hurt the overall US economy. Some of these methods include:

- Keeping labor costs down. This hurts the economy in two ways: 1) lowering government revenue from lower taxes on lower pay, and 2) creating higher unemployment and underemployment, which has led the government to spend more money on services such as unemployment insurance and food stamps.
- Buying back their own stock and reinvesting less in the company, which can hurt them in the medium and long term (Lazonick 2014).

All this behavior leads to higher short-term profits and stock prices but can hurt the medium- and long-term economy. So, in the *Stock Price Economy*, soaring corporate profits and high stock prices may in fact be major obstacles to the true growth of companies and the overall economy.

True growth demands risk—doing something that might fail and consequently decrease profits and the stock price. CEOs, on the other hand, prefer to opt for the practically sure thing: they know that if they can reduce labor and capital costs, the short-term corporate profits and stock prices will increase, and as a result, they will be seen as a success and their compensation will increase. Ultimately, however, the soaring corporate profits and stock prices seen in our current *Stock Price Economy* can be damaging to both US workers and the overall American economy.

Part II

Taxes

CHAPTER 4
Ten Tax Myths That Make the Rich Richer

CHAPTER 5
**Do Half of Americans (Romney's 47%)
Really Pay No Taxes?**

CHAPTER 6.
How the Wealthy Have Dominated Tax Cuts

Chapter 4

Ten Tax Myths That Make the Rich Richer

Ten Tax Myths and Why They Are Untrue

Tax Myth #1: The flat tax is a fair tax.

There is much talk today about instituting a flat tax—that it would only be fair that everyone pay the same federal tax rate on their income. But this wouldn't be the case. The only tax that would be flattened in the flat tax is the tax dominated by the wealthy: the federal income tax (including the marginal long-range capital gains tax, the marginal dividend tax, and the estate tax). On the other hand, the taxes paid heavily by most ordinary Americans—the federal Social Security and Medicare payroll taxes, state taxes, and local taxes—would not be flattened. If a flat tax is instituted, many middle class and other ordinary Americans will pay a higher percentage of their income in total taxes than the wealthy, especially since taxes on financial income is less than half of taxes on earned income. In their approach to using words to make a concept sound better, many on the Right called the flat tax, "the fair tax."

Tax Myth #2: The US is a high-tax country.

Based on all the noise about the so-called high US taxes, one would think that Americans pay among the highest taxes in the world. This is not so. As shown below in Table 6, the US ranks nineteenth and last among the 19 countries with an advanced economy in total taxes as a percentage of GDP. Americans pay a total of 25.5% of GDP in total taxes (including federal income tax, federal payroll taxes, state, and local taxes), compared to an average of 38.5% for the other 18 countries. Considering these facts, the US is absolutely not a high-tax country. Ranked among the countries with an advanced economy, the US is actually an extremely low-tax country.

The other advanced countries spend a lot more money on social and safety net programs than the US does. If one thinks it through, it is the middle class and other non-wealthy citizens who share most of the benefits from these taxes. The rich don't need these social and safety net programs, so the very low taxes in the US are the biggest plus for them. And, with their great political power (through lobbyists, campaign contributions, control of conservative think tanks, etc.), the rich are able to prevail on low taxes and on tax cuts that greatly favor them as an economic group.

Many of the rich would rather not pay for social and safety net programs. Even though such programs provide important benefits to the middle class and other ordinary Americans, acting as a much needed safety net in tough times, they refer to these programs as the "monster" (Woods Jr. 2009).

The Republicans even have a phrase for dealing with the taxes that eventually go for social and safety net programs. They say that it is important to "kill the monster" (President Ronald Reagan used this term) (Reagan, 1987). This is despite the fact that a large majority of people like—even love—these programs once they are in action.

In addition, people in the other advanced countries have important benefits that Americans don't even know about. All the other advanced countries have a minimum number of paid vacation days by law; most have a minimum number of paid sick days by law; and all have a minimum number of paid maternal/paternal leave by law. Americans, on the other hand, have no minimum paid vacation days by law, no minimum paid sick days by law, and no minimum paid days of maternal/paternal leave. As a result, those in other countries with advanced economies take two to three times as many paid vacation days as Americans, and 25% of Americans get no paid vacation days at all; 40% of Americans get no paid sick days at all, and extremely few Americans get paid maternal/paternal leave (Ray, Sanes and Schmitt 2013). At the same time, the US is the only advanced economy in the world not to have universal health care (OECD 2014).

As Table 6 shows, the US is an extremely low total-tax country (OECD 2016):

Table 6
Total Taxes Paid as a Percentage of GDP

Rank	Country	% of GDP Paid in Taxes
1	Denmark	47.6
2	France	45.0
3	Belgium	44.7
4	Italy	43.9
5.5	Finland	43.7
5.5	Sweden	42.7
7	Austria	42.5
8	Norway	40.5
9	Hungary	38.4
10	Netherlands	36.7
11	Germany	36.5
12	Iceland	35.9
13.5	Portugal	34.5
13.5	Greece	34.4
15	United Kingdom	32.9
16	Spain	32.7
17	Canada	30.5
18	Ireland	29
19	United States (all levels)	25.4
	(All countries except the US - mean)	38.5

In 2013, Americans paid 25.4% of their GDP on total taxes compared to an average of 38.5% for people from other countries.

Tax Myth #3: The wealthy are the job creators.

As a result, the Right says that it is dangerous to increase taxes on the wealthy. All this may sound logical, but it is a myth. President Bill Clinton increased the marginal federal income tax rate (paid by the wealthy) from 31% to 39.6%, an increase of 27.7%. The Republicans predicted that this would lead to a deep recession. Instead, the sharp rise in the federal income tax rate for the wealthy was followed by a very long economic expansion, and the net development of more than 22 million new jobs during Clinton's eight-year administration, and the highest increase in real wages since Reagan became president (Waldman 2014).

On the other hand, when President George W. Bush cut the marginal federal income tax rate from 39.6% to 35%, reduced the long-range capital gains tax to 15%, reduced the Dividend Tax from the regular federal income marginal rate (39.6%) to 15%, and sharply cut the Estate tax—all taxes that the wealthy (top 1%) pay heavily, the Bush expansion that ensued was the weakest recovery since the Great Depression and was followed by the financial crash and the Great Recession at the end of Bush's administration (Dubay 2013). I have a very different view than the Republicans/Right Wing about who the job creators are.

Consumers account for about two-thirds of the US economy, and too many Americans don't make enough money from their jobs to buy what they need and want. Basically, our economy is choking its customers, creating what I call a "demand" problem. It is no coincidence that the US economy generally prospered when the middle class was strong and were paid relatively well for their work. When American workers receive decent pay for their work, it not only helps solve their personal economic problems, it helps solve the problem of demand in the overall US economy.

Tax Myth #4: Republicans say that when people complain about too much Income Inequality, they are causing "class warfare."

Warren Buffett, the multi-billionaire investor, has said that a class war has already taken place in the US, and that his class (the rich) has won (Sargent 2011). It takes a great deal of chutzpah for politicians (who have won this battle in favor of the rich) to accuse those who question what actually happened, and to blame them for fomenting class war and pitting class against class. When the Right Wing claims that the liberals/socialists/etc. only want to redistribute income from the rich to other Americans, they should remember that for more than 30 years the reverse has been true: money has been redistributed from average Americans to the rich, and that this redistribution is now speeding up, especially since the Great Recession. It is not that liberals want to switch wealth to the middle class; they hope the government will create a system whereby the middle class and other ordinary people get their rightful share of American prosperity.

Tax Myth #5: Republican presidents have always been tax cutters.
Not true. When Dwight Eisenhower, the two-term Republican president, began his term, the marginal federal income tax rate was 91%; when he left, eight years later, it was still 91%. It was a Democratic president, John F. Kennedy, who reduced the marginal federal income tax rate from 91% to 70%, which is still high (Fowler 2011). Neither of the next two Republican presidents, Richard Nixon and Gerald Ford, were big tax cutters either—nor was the Democratic president, Jimmy Carter.

It was only when Ronald Reagan became president that the Republicans became the big tax cut political party—especially cuts beneficial for the wealthy. Actually, Reagan's tax cuts were so large that he eventually had to increase taxes (Sahadi 2010). And the next Republican president George H.W. Bush got himself into big trouble with his own political party—he promised not to increase taxes, with his famous "read my lips" quote, but then had to raise taxes because of the huge deficit they caused (Barber 2014).

It is amazing to me that the US marginal federal income tax rate decreased only from 91% to 70% from 1948 to 1980—a period of 32 years—yet, in only two terms (eight years), President Reagan reduced the marginal federal income tax rate from 70% to 28%. In other words, the marginal income tax rate lowered by 21% in 32 years, and then in just eight years, President Reagan reduced it by 42%. Following Reagan, President George W. Bush was also a major tax cutter—again, as mentioned earlier, favoring the wealthy (Tax Foundation 2013).

Many Republican presidents (since the 1930s) weren't ardent tax cutters, but they definitely are today—and the tax cuts greatly favor the wealthy. Presidents Reagan and Bush didn't appear overly concerned about how the cuts would cause massive budget deficits. It seems that the Right Wing worries about such deficits only during Democratic administrations.

Tax Myth #6: The American people don't want to tax the rich.

Again, a myth. Americans were recently asked what they believed should be the primary way to balance the federal budget: 61% thought the rich should be taxed more; 4% thought the Medicare program should be cut; 3% thought the Social Security program should be cut; and 20% thought the Defense budget should be cut. Even Tea Party adherents were against reducing the Medicare program by a margin of more than two to one.

Americans generally believe that they will need the two programs, Social Security and Medicare, when they retire. The large majority of Republicans, including Tea Party adherents, don't expect to become moguls, and thus believe they will need to take advantage of the two government programs in their later years. The data also suggest that, despite the propaganda being used by the Right, most Americans believe that these two programs will be there for them when they reach 65.

Tax Myth #7: Social Security is a major financial problem.

This is not the case. In 2009, because the Social Security payroll taxes taken in were $147 billion higher than the Social Security benefits expended, if there were no Social Security program, the budget deficit for 2009 would have had to be announced as $147 billion higher than was the case (Social Security Administration 2009).

At the end of 2009, the Social Security Trust Fund had a total of $2.5 trillion (with a "t") in it (Social Security Administration 2009), and it is estimated that this figure will grow to $2.9 trillion in a decade. If there were no Social Security program, the total budget deficit would have had to be announced as $2.5 trillion more than had been announced in 2009, and $2.9 trillion more than will be announced in 2019.

The money collected by the government in Social Security payroll taxes has been much higher than the Social Security benefits given to recipients. Also, even those who want to reduce the Social Security program admit that with no changes in the program, it will be able to pay full benefits for the next 21 years (until 2037).

Since this situation goes back to when the Greenspan Social Security Commission of 1983 developed the current program, this means that by 2037, the program will have remained constant for more than 50 years.

Even the so-called 75-year debt of Social Security, which is treated as a fact, is only a shaky estimation, based on a 75-year estimation of the US's economic growth, which is much lower than the actual economic growth of the last 75 years. The group that oversees Social Security also developed two other estimates to show that it is very difficult to do a 75-year estimate and be correct. One of the two other estimates predicts that the growth rate will be higher than the one discussed above but still lower than the past 75-year growth rate (Goss 2010). Using that estimate, there would be no need to change anything indefinitely: no increase in the Social Security payroll tax, no decrease in Social Security benefits, no increase in the age of eligibility, etc. So, just what is the rush to change Social Security in a way that would hurt its recipients?

Tax Myth #8: The estate tax is a "death" tax.
Not true—the estate tax is a wealth tax. It is collected at death because that is when the size of the estate can best be calculated. Politicians like Theodore Roosevelt and Franklin Roosevelt favored the estate tax, saying it was good both for the government and for those receiving the bequest, because they would be more involved in life. They also felt that in a democracy, it would be unfair for some to begin their lives with millions or billions of dollars, while some begin their lives with nothing. Even Adam Smith, the father of capitalism, said that he found it difficult to defend leaving money to a child, other than to a child with a problem that needed long-term care.

Calling the estate tax a "death tax" is an example of the Republican approach of selecting terms that are misleading but excellent from a marketing point-of-view. Yet, the Democrats have not been able to effectively counter this concept.

Tax Myth #9: Cutting the marginal federal income tax rate from 39.6% to 23%, and removing loopholes worth that amount to the wealthy (the Bowles-Simpson plan) is a fair thing to do.
This is certainly a myth. The tax bill of 1986 supposedly took the loopholes out

of the tax code, yet here they are once again. The wealthy simply use their lobbyists and campaign contributions to press Congress to insert the loopholes (sometimes under another name) back into the tax code. What doesn't change is the huge marginal percentage tax cut. In the case of the Bowles-Simpson Commission, there would be a huge cut in the marginal federal income tax rate—from 39.6% to 23% (McBride 2012). (The marginal federal income tax rate was 91% until 1960.) The government keeps finding ways to reduce the taxes of the wealthy.

The wealthy spend millions on lobbying and get paid off in billions. Eventually, other Americans have to pay for it and/or it adds to the deficit. One example is the current conventional wisdom that it is important to reduce the benefits of the entitlements, such as Social Security, Medicare, and Medicaid. If the taxes of the wealthy had not been cut so much in the past, there would be no need to even think about decreasing the benefits of the entitlements.

Tax Myth #10. The US corporate tax rate is too high.
Despite the fact that the nominal corporate rate of 35% is high, companies simply don't pay that amount. Actual corporate taxes have fallen precipitously:

- In recent decades, corporate tax revenue has fallen sharply, from 6% of GDP in the 1950s to 2% today, due to a proliferation of tax loopholes and the use of offshore havens (the concept of tax havens have made Bermuda and the Cayman Islands famous—or infamous) (Pomerleau 2014). In fact, according to the Congressional Budget Office, corporate tax receipts as a share of corporate profits have hit their lowest point in 40 years (Paletta 2012).
- According to the Congressional Budget Office, total corporate federal taxes have fallen to 12.1% of profits earned from activities within the US in fiscal 2011—less than half the 25.6% average from 1987 to 2008, and significantly lower than the supposed 35% tax on profits they are supposed to pay (Paletta 2012).
- At the same time that corporations are pulling in huge amounts of money, workers are seeing their wages sink. Even after the Great Recession officially ended, real wages fell. A major part of the reason why business

profits are so high is that business sees it as a zero-sum game, with labor on the losing end.

- Cutting the corporate income tax rate would not spur economic growth (i.e., there is no evidence that changes in either the nominal corporate tax rate or the effective corporate tax rate has led to economic growth).

Following is a list of how some major companies have used accounting and other tricks to sharply cut corporate taxes—sometimes paying no corporate taxes at all:

- Apple used a complicated system of international subsidies and cost shifting to save $74 billion in corporate taxes from 2009 to 2012 (O'Toole 2013).
- Microsoft saved $7 billion of its US tax bill in 2009 by using loopholes to lower its taxes (Liberto 2012).
- Hewlett-Packard avoided paying taxes through a series of loans shifting billions of dollars between two offshore subsidies.
- In 2010, General Electric reported worldwide profits of $14.2 billion, including $5.1 billion from the US. It paid no taxes to the US at all; in fact, GE claimed a tax benefit of $3.2 billion (Kocieniewski 2011).
- The most popular corporate tax cutting method today is tax inversion, where companies purchase a smaller business in another (low-tax) country, incorporate in the low-tax country, and pay the lower taxes of the smaller country. The companies not only pay low taxes in the other country, but they also stop paying taxes to the US altogether (Eichelberger and Gilson 2015).

Chapter 5

Do Half of Americans (Romney's 47%) Really Pay No Taxes?

In the run-up to the 2012 presidential election, Mitt Romney's claim that half of Americans (47%) pay no taxes and thus favor Obama for president may have cost him the election, but it is the conventional wisdom of the Republicans and Right Wing that they don't. Romney isn't the first person to make this claim—many on the Right already have.

Is Romney's Claim True?

It is mostly true that 47% of Americans pay no federal income tax and that the wealthy (top 1%) pay 38% of all federal income tax (Farley 2012). However, both claims are based on a trick. The federal income tax accounts for only 25.5% of the total tax collected in the US (2011 figures) (US Government Revenue 2011). The federal payroll taxes (the Social Security payroll tax and the Medicare payroll tax), state taxes, and local taxes account for about three-quarters of all taxes collected in the US, and the middle class and other ordinary Americans pay a lot of these taxes. This results in some ordinary Americans paying higher total tax rates than the wealthy. Note that Romney paid below 15% of his income on his 2010 federal income tax return (Farley 2012). In another recent tax year, Romney had to forego declaring his charitable contributions in order to get his tax rate above 10% (Kucinich and McCoy 2012).

Since taxes other than federal income taxes account for a very small percentage of the income of the wealthy, it is very possible for average Americans to pay a higher percentage of their income on total taxes than someone like Romney. This would not be that unusual. The extremely rich Warren Buffet has said that he pays a lower tax rate on his income than anyone in his office, including his secretary (Isidore 2013). The main reason is that the tax rate on financial income (which the rich dominate) is less than half the marginal tax rate on earned income.

Total Taxes Paid as a Percentage of Income

Table 7 shows the percent of income paid in total taxes by income category:

Table 7
Percentage of Income Paid in (Total) Taxes

Income Group	Percentage of Income Paid in (Total) Taxes
Top 1%	29%
Next 4%	30.4%
Next 5%	30.3%
Next 10%	29.5%
Fourth 20%	28.3%
Middle 20% (Median)	25.2%
Second 20%	21.2%
Lowest 20%	17.4%

Two Major Points from Table 7:

1. The bottom 47% in household income may pay no federal income tax, but they pay a lot of total taxes. For example, the bottom 40% of Americans in income pay an average of 19.3% of their income in (total) taxes—certainly not "no taxes" as claimed by many on the Right. In fact, these people at the bottom of our economy may pay a higher tax rate than some millionaires and billionaires do, especially in states that do not have a state tax. It may be a long time since Romney has paid a total tax of 19.3% on his income.

2. While wealthy households (top 1%) pay a very high 38% of the total federal income taxes collected, they pay only a little higher (total) tax rate on their incomes as median Americans (29% to 25%).

Two Untrue Claims about Taxes That Must Be Rectified

There are major consequences to allowing the conventional wisdom to remain that:

1. Half of Americans do not pay any taxes.
2. The wealthy (top 1%) pay far more of their income in taxes than do average Americans.

Implications of Allowing the Conventional Wisdom to Remain as Perceived Truths:

First, because it's believed by many that close to half of Americans pay no tax, there is some call, led by those on the Right, for a tax change that would increase the percentage of Americans who pay the federal income tax, which today does not include the poorest half of Americans. In polling, most Americans think that the federal budget should be balanced by increasing the taxes of the wealthy, but this option is not on the table of those in power, even the leaders of the Democratic Party. To a major degree, those in charge of both political parties do not listen carefully to the middle class or to other ordinary Americans—which is why the middle class needs a nonpolitical organization that fights for their economic needs.

Second, it allows the Right to distract from the desire of Americans to increase taxes on the wealthy. Generally, Americans are not the rugged individualists that conventional wisdom suggests they are, and they don't believe they will become rich—on the contrary, they believe they will need Social Security and Medicare when they become seniors. This is why polls show that even the Right strongly believes that Social Security and Medicare should be kept as is. Even two-thirds of the Tea Party adherents, the most Right Wing of the Right Wing, have this opinion (On the Issues 2012). The idea may go against their ideology, but people don't want to live in poverty when they are older.

Third, the current perception of many Right Wingers is that Americans back the development of a flat tax, often called a fair tax (Shlaes 2015). However, the flat tax would be extremely unfair to the middle class and other ordinary Americans, as the only tax that would truly be "flattened" is the federal income tax, which the wealthy dominate. (This was also discussed in the previous chapter, "Ten Tax Myths That Make the Rich Richer.")

Chapter 6

How the Wealthy Have Dominated the Tax Cuts

Taxes Cut to Benefit the Wealthy (Top 1%) under Presidents Reagan and Bush

Tax cuts made since 1980 have essentially been instituted to benefit the wealthy, a group that would normally pay a much higher tax rate than average Americans (traditionally, American tax rates have been progressive). The tax rates that have been cut sharply since 1980 are listed below:

- The marginal federal income tax: Lowered from 70% to 35%
- The long-term capital gains tax: Lowered to 15%
- The dividend tax: Lowered from 35% (which is now the regular marginal federal income tax rate) to 15%
- The Estate tax: Sharply lowered (both the size of the estate required for eligibility, and the percentage that has to be paid of the estate), and some say it should be repealed completely

Taxes on Earned Income versus Unearned Income

The reason why a billionaire like Warren Buffet can pay a tax rate lower than his secretary and why former Republican presidential nominee Romney can pay a tax rate of 15% or less on his annual income of many millions is because the US tax rates on financial income (from dividends, capital gains, etc.) are less than half the tax rates on earned income (from a job).

Yet, Andrew Mellon, essentially the father of the supply-side thinking in economics, who cut taxes in the 1920s as much as President Reagan in the 1980s, believed that earned income (from a job) should be taxed at a lower rate than unearned income (from investments). As Mellon argued in his book, *Taxation: the People's Business*, published in 1924 (Mellon 1924):

"The fairness of taxing more lightly income from wages, salaries than from investments is beyond question. In the first case, the income is uncertain and limited in duration; sickness or death destroys it and old age diminishes it; in the other, the source of income continues; the income may be disposed of during a man's life and it descends to his heirs."

"Surely we can afford to make a distinction between the people whose only capital is their mettle and physical energy and the people whose income is derived from investments. Such a distinction would mean much to millions of American workers and would be an added inspiration to the man who must provide a competence during his few productive years for himself and his family when his earnings capacity is at an end."

Yet, our tax code allows the wealthy (top 1%) to pay a tax rate in which unearned income is not only taxed less than the marginal earned income tax rate but less than half as much.

The supply-siders, who swear by Andrew Mellon and his supply-side argument, have forgotten to remind Americans of the other side of Mellon's argument. They have also forgotten to give us his argument in favor of the progressive income tax and his opinion that in times of financial distress—like the Depression (or perhaps war)—money must be raised and so taxes would have to be increased.

Mellon believed most strongly in a balanced budget and never would have gone along with the Ronald Reagan and George W. Bush tax cuts, both of which caused enormous budget deficits. President George W. Bush is the first American president to cut taxes during a war (Brownstein 2003). It would appear that today's supply-siders stress only those aspects of Andrew Mellon's philosophy that favor the economic well-being of the wealthy.

Cutting the tax rate for the wealthy has been a conscious objective from the beginning for those who made these tax cuts. David Stockman, Reagan's budget director and lead man on his first tax cuts has admitted in an interview with a reporter from *The Atlantic* magazine that the major objective of Reagan's first financial plan was always to cut the marginal rate on the federal income tax rate (Greider 1981). Eventually, Reagan cut the marginal rate on the federal income tax from 70% to 28%, an amazing 60% reduction on a tax dominated by the rich. Again, the middle class and other ordinary Americans pay most of their taxes on the federal payroll taxes (on Social Security and Medicare), state taxes, and local taxes, which weren't cut.

Part III

American Attitudes toward Big Government Programs

CHAPTER 7
Does the Government Subsidize Social Security?

CHAPTER 8
How Do Americans Really Feel about Big Government Programs?

Does the Government Subsidize Social Security?

How the (False) Social Security Crisis Took Place

It is commonly believed that Social Security is in a financial crisis and that it has made the US financial condition worse. As such, there is now essentially an agreement between the Right and many "moderate" Democrats to, in one way or another, cut Social Security benefits. (I will explain in this chapter why this doesn't make sense.)

When George W. Bush began his second term, he said that he would use the political capital he gained from winning the 2004 election to privatize the Social Security program—because it was in a financial crisis. The privatization approach went down to ignominious defeat, but somehow, despite being incorrect, the crisis part of Bush's approach stuck and has become part of the conventional wisdom.

Not Even Close to a State of Crisis

The conventional wisdom is that if the US wants to be serious about cutting its huge budget deficit, it must reduce the cost of the Social Security program. However, Social Security is not in a financial crisis at all. Even those who want to cut Social Security costs admit the program will pay full benefits for 21 years (until 2037) without any change in Social Security payroll taxes, benefits paid, or age of eligibility (Social Security Administration 2016). In fact, Social Security received more in payroll taxes than it distributed in Social Security benefits for nearly 30 years since the 1983 Greenspan Social Security Commission set the new rates of payroll taxes and benefits, and its reserves will last until 2034 (Desilver 2015).

A Financial Safety Valve If Funds Are Needed

Even if or when the Social Security Trust Fund ever does run out of money, the Social Security program won't be bankrupt. Social Security recipients would still be paid about 75% of full benefits out of current (at that time) Social Security payroll taxes. But I don't believe this will be necessary. In 1983, Social Security encountered a financial problem, which was fixed in a year by the Greenspan Social Security Commission (Martin and Weaver 2005). If necessary, a new Social Security Commission can relatively quickly make adjustments.

The So-Called "Crisis" Partially Based on an Accounting Trick

The concern about Social Security being in a financial crisis is, to an important degree, based on an accounting trick. Those who believe in the crisis claim that the government pays 20% of the US budget on Social Security benefits—which it does (Center on Budget and Policy Initiatives 2015). However, the government also collects more in Social Security payroll taxes (including interest on the bonds in the Social Security Trust Fund) than it pays out in benefits. The accounting trick that allows the opponents of Social Security to claim there's a crisis is the fact that they consider the benefits paid as Social Security expenses but don't consider the money received from the Social Security payroll tax as Social Security income—shocking, but true.

Another Trick Placing Social Security in a False Crisis

The Social Security Trust Fund is made up of payroll taxes that haven't yet been spent, plus bonds from money in the Social Security Trust Fund, which have the same full faith of the US government as do other US government bonds. The interest on the bonds is the same as that given on bonds purchased at that time by Americans, foreign countries, or anyone else.

The accounting trick is to consider that the Social Security Trust Fund bonds should get no interest. With that approach, the Social Security program does have a deficit. However, not only does the US government regard the bonds in the Trust Fund with the same full faith as other US bonds, but if the Social Security Trust Fund (paid by Americans who pay the Social Security payroll tax) didn't loan the US government the money, the government would have had to sell more bonds to China, etc., and there wouldn't be any question about whether or not to pay the interest. In conclusion, from a legal and moral point of view alike, the government bonds in the Social Security Trust Fund should be treated like all other bonds of the US government.

The Social Security Program: Reducing, not Increasing, the US Budget Deficit

If there were no Social Security program, the US would have had to announce significantly higher budget deficits than it has thus far.

- **Lowering the Deficit by $121 Billion in 2009.** In 2009, the government paid approximately $562 billion dollars in Social Security benefits. However, it received about $709 billion in Social Security payroll taxes (including interest from the bonds in the Social Security Trust Fund). Thus, in 2009, Social Security afforded the US government a $147 billion surplus. If there were no Social Security program, the budget deficit for 2009 would have had to be announced as $147 billion higher than was announced.
- **Making a $2.9 Trillion Difference by 2019.** At the end of 2009, there was about $2.5 trillion (with a "t") in the Social Security Trust Fund (the surplus of Social Security payroll taxes taken in over Social Security benefits paid out, plus the money earned from government bonds in the Trust Fund; i.e., bonds purchased with money from the Trust Fund). Also, another $400 billion is expected to be added to the Social Security Trust Fund in the next decade, for a total of $2.9 trillion.

If there were no Social Security program, the government would have had to announce a total budget deficit at the end of 2009 that was $2.5 trillion higher than they did. If there were no Social Security program, the budget deficit announced in 2019 would have to be announced as $2.9 trillion (with a "t") higher than would have to be announced if there were no Social Security program. Of course, the money has been saved in the Social Security Fund because the actuaries of the Greenspan Committee were aware that costs of the program would increase over time—that the number of people who are beneficiaries would grow relative to those still working and paying the Social Security payroll taxes and that people would live longer in the future. (One reason for the difficulty in understanding the effect of payroll taxes on the budget deficit is that for a long time now, Social Security payroll taxes have been mixed in with the general budget. They shouldn't be.)

Sometimes, announced budget surpluses aren't really surpluses. The budget treats the money collected from payroll taxes as regular income, which is incorrect. However, US presidents like this idea because it lowers deficits and sometimes even shows a budget surplus when there really isn't one. To American presidents, this is "free money."

Another Significant Plus—Social Security Helping to Create Demand

In tough economic times, Social Security is good for the overall US economy for an additional reason. We've already discussed that the US economy has a "demand" problem. People don't have enough money to buy the products and services they need and/or would like to buy. Since Social Security recipients generally have low incomes, they tend to spend their Social Security benefits quickly, which helps solve the "demand" problem. Taking away or reducing the Social Security program would remove that flow of money into the economy, and the "demand" problem would be significantly worse.

The 75-Year Estimated Deficit: Only a Projection, but Treated as a Fact

Many warn that the Social Security program will have a program deficit in 75 years (Goss 2010). This is spoken about as if it were a fact, but it is not. It is merely an estimate based on the projected US economic growth over the next 75 years. One should note that the approximated increase of US growth used to arrive at this 75-year deficit is much lower than growth has actually proven to be for the past 75 years. The group that oversees Social Security has also computed an estimate of future growth that is higher than this first one, but still lower than the growth of the past 75 years. With that estimate, full

Social Security benefits can be paid ad infinitum, with no change in the program. The overseers of the Social Security program produced three estimates in order to communicate that any estimate can be wrong—indeed is likely to be wrong. In any case, what's the rush in cutting the Social Security program?

Can Social Security Recipients Afford a Cut in Benefits?

A critical question I haven't seen asked is, "Can recipients afford a cut in Social Security benefits?" See what you think:

- Including Social Security benefits, one out of three recipients (33%) gets all or nearly all (90% to 100%) of their income from Social Security; two out of three recipients (65%) get most of their income from Social Security benefits (Chapman and Ettlinger 2005).
- Including Social Security benefits, 21% of recipients have an income of $10,000 a year or less; 61% (three out of five) have an annual income of $25,000 or less (all in real dollars)

Many—Perhaps Most—Recipients Cannot Afford a Cut in Benefits

With such low incomes, I don't think that many, and perhaps most, Social Security recipients can afford to have their benefits reduced. It is shameful that this issue has not been at the forefront of the Social Security debate of whether to cut the benefits of the most successful program the US has ever instituted—a program that has reduced the percentage of seniors living below the poverty level from about 50% to less than 10%. Do we really want to increase the number of American seniors living in poverty? Do we really want to increase the number of American seniors living without dignity? These seniors have paid significant Social Security taxes for all their working lives. Also, research shows that if their employers hadn't paid their share of the Social Security taxes, most of this money would have gone to the workers in the form of wage increases. There are much better ways to get money for the program if necessary. One obvious approach would be to have Americans pay Social Security payroll taxes on all their income instead of stopping their payments at an income of just over $100,000.

The Collapse of the Defined Benefit Pension Programs

What makes the idea of cutting the Social Security benefits situation much worse is that the number of defined benefit plans, which employers usually pay, has fallen by 62% from 1974–1975 to 2003–2004, while the number of defined contribution plans (including 401Ks) that most employees must pay for mostly or entirely by themselves has increased by 223% from 1974–1975 to 2003–2004.

The 401K Never Intended as a Pension

A problem with using a 401K as a substitute for a pension (or Social Security) is that the psychology of a 401 K (similar to buying stocks in general) is to buy when the market is high and sell when the market is low.

It is also the case that 401K owners often put money in a 401K when times are good and stock prices are high (and people tend to be optimistic); they often don't when times are not as good (and they are feeling pessimistic). All this results in poor investment results. People like Warren Buffett understand the psychology of buying and selling stock, and act upon it, which is a major reason why they so successful in investing, but most people fall prey to the two investing problems.

Those who retired when the market fell drastically during the Great Recession would have been in a terrible bind if Social Security had been privatized, as George W. Bush had attempted to do. Actually, the 401K was never meant to be a pension, but rather, as something extra that people could put away.

Probably the first rule of pensions, especially as people get older, is not to put risky investments into it. The huge preponderance of Americans do not have the skill set necessary to do this well. The people who would make a huge amount of money if Social Security were privatized reside in the Wall Street community—the brokers, mutual fund administrators, etc. who would handle the transactions made by the owners of privatized Social Security accounts.

Social Security Not Really an Entitlement but a Funded Annuity Plan

One reason I believe those who wish to reduce the benefits of the Social Security system "think they can get away with it" is that Social Security is called an "entitlement," a term with the connotation of being "something for nothing." It is important to realize that Social Security is not an entitlement but, essentially, a paid-for annuity plan. People have been paying for it all their working lives and it would be more aptly titled the Social Security Annuity Plan. Those who dislike the Social Security plan find it far too easy to rail against it when it is called "an "entitlement." I think they would have more of a problem pushing the Social Security program around if "Annuity Plan" were officially part of the name.

Increasing the Age of Eligibility: An Across-the-Board Reduction of Benefits

There is much talk that rather than cut Social Security benefits, the age of eligibility should be increased. This is yet another accounting trick. Increasing the age of eligibility by one year means an across-the-board, 5% decrease in Social Security benefits per year—or one out of approximately 20 years of Social Security benefits (averaging the data for men and women). The average couple on Social Security gets approximately $25,000 a year in Social Security benefits (Social Security Administration 2015). This means that the average couple would receive $50,000 less if the eligibility age is increased by two years, as most proposed changes suggest.

Increasing the age of eligibility may not seem like a decrease in Social Security benefits, but it absolutely is. Some people have suggested that the age of eligibility be put off for four years, to 70 years old. This would amount to an across-the-board decrease of benefits of 20%. Putting off the age of eligibility to 70 would amount to $100,000 less in a couple's benefits. Many Americans are already putting off their medical needs, waiting for the Medicare eligibility age of 65. Putting off care even longer could mean worse health results or even put their lives at risk. Raising the Social Security and Medicare eligibility age by two or four years would likely force hundreds of thousands (or even millions) more Americans to put off their health needs for that period, which could have dire results as already discussed. These people would have to put off this medical care for even more years than they do now.

Some Important Thoughts about Social Security:

1. The Social Security program is safe for at least 21 years. Even those who want to cut Social Security admit it will go until 2037 paying Social Security payments with absolutely no changes in the program. There really should be no rush to change it now.

2. Those who want to cut the Social Security problem warn that people are living longer and that the ratio between the numbers of workers paying payroll taxes to the number of Social Security recipients is falling. The actuaries in the 1983 Greenspan Social Security Commission were aware of this likelihood, and this is the major reason that $2.5 trillion is saved in the Social Security Trust Fund, and that more money is expected to be added in the next decade.

3. The chances of a 75-year estimate based on other estimates being correct are slim to none. It is certainly not a fact, though it is treated as if it were.

4. A poll shows that 61% of Americans think that the primary way to balance the budget should be to increase the taxes on the rich, compared to only 4% who say the Social Security program should be cut, and only 3% who say that the Medicare program should be cut (20% say the US Department of Defense budget should be reduced). Why is nobody listening to the American people (and the American voters)? Instead, if or when more money is needed for the Social Security program, why not have Americans pay Social Security payroll taxes on their total income? The powers that be are simply not listening to the American people.

Chapter 8

How Do Americans Really Feel about Big Government Programs?

Americans' Paradoxical Feelings toward Big Government Programs

The paradox: many Americans see themselves as conservative, yet the programs they support— often very much—are big government, even liberal programs. About 70% of the Tea Party adherents (the most Right Wing of the Right Wing) want to see Medicare, probably the most fiscally risky government program, continue as is. They also want the Social Security program to remain as it is (On the Issues 2012).

In this chapter we examine American attitudes towards quite a few big government programs, including both social and safety net programs. Paradoxically, after many of these Big Government, liberal programs proved they were working successfully, a large majority of Americans, often including many so-called conservatives, become very much in favor of them. Furthermore, I believe that if Americans knew they were available, they would probably appreciate other social and safety net programs that all—or nearly all—people in other advanced countries enjoy as well. The tendency of many conservatives, however, is to question these bills for large government programs when they are initially offered, and to approve of them only after they have seen the results, especially when many millions of dollars of false propaganda act to "demonize" them.

It is just as important, perhaps more important, to effectively communicate to Americans that the Right wants to reduce—even repeal—some of the programs that will greatly improve their lives and help them if and when they hit a rough patch in their life, as most of us do. For example, even though Americans approve of Medicare and have made it clear that it is important to them, a Republican budget that Paul Ryan first introduced in 2011 would change Medicare as we know it. Instead of simply covering seniors' medical costs when they are sick (with some copays, etc.), the budget would change their coverage to a voucher. Seniors would be given a certain amount of money and have to purchase their own private healthcare plan. It could be that some seniors would not be able to afford this healthcare.

As Ryan attempted to privatize healthcare, Bush similarly tried hard to privatize Social Security. If he had succeeded, it would have spelled disaster for those who retired at that time, because the stock market crashed.

The Idea of "Big Government Programs" Often Demonized by the Right

This subject is much discussed today. I think that the conventional wisdom is that most Americans are Center-Right. For example, polling has shown that for a number of years, one-and-a-half times as many Americans describe themselves as conservative than as liberal. The rest consider themselves neither.

In his First Inaugural Address, Reagan said: "Government is not the solution to our problem; government is the problem"—an anti-Big-Government saying if there ever was one (Reagan 1981). And even Democratic President Bill Clinton was quoted as saying: "The era of big government is over," a statement some might say at least heads towards the Right (Clinton 1996).

However, I think that the best way to think about the questions posed in this chapter is in two parts: 1) what people say they want hypothetically, and 2) how they feel about specific programs after they have been instituted for a while.

A major factor in why Americans say they don't like Big Government programs is the propaganda and lobbying on which many millions of dollars are spent. Between attempts by the government to institute a government healthcare program, polls show that two-thirds of Americans believe that everyone should be guaranteed healthcare insurance, with those who can't afford to buy it being subsidized. But the hundreds of millions of dollars worth of propaganda has changed attitudes, probably temporarily I suspect.

Most American people may say they are politically conservative, yet, they favor the large majority of programs that are Big Government, even liberal programs. Table 8 shows the results of a 2005 Kaiser Family Foundation Poll. This table shows the percentage of respondents who rate various social programs as "very important" (The Kaiser Family Foundation 2005):

Table 8
Percentage of Americans Who Rate Program "Very Important"

Program	Percentage Who Rate Program as Very Important
Social Security	88%
Medicare	83%
Medicaid	74%
Loans for college studies	65%
Defense, military spending	57%
Foreign aid	20%

1. Social Security

Social Security may be the most successful Big Government, even liberal program ever. It has resulted in reducing the percentage of seniors living in poverty by over 70%—from 35% to under 10% (Romig 2008). Thus, it is no surprise that 88% of Americans—nearly 9 out of 10—rated it as being "very important," even though tens of millions of Americans are decades away from being eligible for Social Security and the majority of Americans say they are conservative.

2. Medicare

Medicare in the future may be a major financial problem for the US, but it is also a liberal, Big Government program that is appreciated by a huge majority of the American people, 83% rating it as "very important." Even two-thirds of Tea Party adherents want to keep Medicare as is. This is why the Middle-Class Organization we recommend should be apolitical. Many Republicans, even those from the Tea Party, would be likely to favor the new organization if it were nonpolitical.

There is no question that Medicare poses a financial problem, but I think that this is really a healthcare cost problem, not a Medicare problem. The US spends twice as much per capita for healthcare as the average advanced country (Kane 2012), yet has about 30 million citizens who still are uninsured—a mediocre result compared with the other countries with advanced economies, all of which have universal healthcare systems (The Kaiser Commission on Medicaid and the Uninsured 2015).

A relatively recent poll shows how important Americans think Social Security and Medicare are. In the poll, Americans were asked which of the following they thought should be the primary way to balance the US budget deficit: increasing taxes on the rich, reducing defense spending, or reducing the Social Security or Medicare budgets. There may be a great deal of criticism of the latter two entitlement programs by the Republicans and the Right Wing, but very, very few Americans think that reducing these entitlement programs should be the primary solution to a budget deficit. Table 9 shows the results of the poll (Cooke 2011):

Table 9
The Best Way to Balance the Budget

Increase taxes on the rich	61%
Reduce defense spending	20%
Reduce the Medicare program	4%
Reduce the Social Security Program	3%

Interestingly, a large majority of Americans think that the primary way to balance the budget would be to tax the rich more. Indeed, the history of taxes since 1980 has been to tax the rich much less than used to be the case. Their taxes have been cut sharply. But there is at least one simple way to have the rich pay more for Social Security if and when there is a need for more money for the program. As mentioned earlier, if funds are necessary, Americans can simply pay the Social Security payroll tax on their entire income, rather than just the first $100,000+. The wealthy would be paying more, but they can afford to do so, and it is what the American people say they want.

However, this approach doesn't seem to be on the table for Social Security. What is on the table are a number of ways to reduce Social Security benefits. It appears that Washington is not really listening to the people. But this is not surprising since middle-class and other ordinary Americans do not have the money to hire lobbyists or make large political contributions.

All this reminds me of a television news story of a woman attending a Tea Party demonstration. She was carrying a sign that said: "Keep the government out of my Medicare." When she was told that Medicare was a government program, she got upset and thought that maybe it should remain as is.

It may be that many Americans are not aware that all, or nearly all, of the social and safety net programs they count on and love are Big Government programs, usually opposed by the Republicans and the Right Wing when they were first considered, and that the latter two groups (Republicans and Right Wingers, though they often overlap) even today want to reduce some of these programs or even repeal them.

Regarding the strategy of the 2016 elections, I would like to stress that if Americans elect a Republican president, they should prepare to see Medicare, Social Security, and other programs they care about reduced or even repealed.

3. Medicaid

Medicaid is rated as "very important" by 74% of Americans, somewhat lower than the ratings for Social Security or Medicare. If I had to guess why, I would say that it is because Medicare and Social Security are offered to all Americans, while Medicaid was designed to ensure that the poor get healthcare. Most people probably don't realize that much, possibly most, of the Medicaid money is spent for long-term nursing home care for seniors. Still, the fact that 74% of Americans rate Medicaid as "very important" indicates that the large majority of Americans favor the Medicaid program.

4. Loans for College Students

Loans for college students have become a big financial problem for both the students and the government. Many students graduate with major debts and, in these difficult economic times, college graduates often cannot get a job in the area in which they were trained. Instead, some are unemployed and many are forced to take low-wage service jobs—and those with student loans cannot even negate the loan if they go into bankruptcy. This is a huge problem for millions who attend or have attended college recently. In any case, many Americans find it problematic to get on with their lives because they first have to pay back their student loans.

The size of the problem is clearly visible by the fact that there is more student loan credit out there than credit card debt—about $1.3 trillion worth (Market Watch 2016). Still, about two-out-of-three (65%) Americans are in favor of the student debt program. Likely, most Americans believe that all American boys and girls should have a chance to go to college if they think it will improve their circumstances in life.

5. Permanent Disability Insurance

This isn't a separate program—it's part of Social Security. So, Social Security is both a pension and a permanent disability program. I have not seen this issue polled, but I would be shocked if the large majority of Americans were not in favor of it—after all, a permanent disability can happen to anyone. The Permanent Disability pension is also a Big Government program.

6. FHA/Veteran's Mortgages

From FDR on, the Democrats have tried to give homeowners a break, offering a slightly lower home mortgage cost that assists both the American people and the housing industry. This not only saves the homeowner interest costs, but most likely increases the value of the house. I have not seen quantitative information on this issue, but the program is in all likelihood a favorite with most Americans.

7. Mortgage Tax Deductions

Again, the government favors the homeowner, as mortgage taxes are deductible from the income tax. This not only saves homeowners a lot of money, it also likely increases the value of the home. Again, I don't remember seeing polling on the matter, but offering a tax deduction is in the interest of home-owners, which is the majority of Americans. Again, this is a Big Government program, but who would be against a mortgage deduction? Even so, there is much talk about eliminating this deduction.

8. Minimum Wage

Two years into the Bill Clinton administration, Congress took up a bill that would increase the minimum wage. I saw a poll on the subject and was surprised by the results. Following up, I asked my daughter—who is generally aware of what's happening but doesn't follow politics as closely as I do—what percentage of Americans did she think would be in favor of increasing the minimum wage? Her guess was that relatively few would favor the new bill, so she was very surprised when I told her the results of the poll.

My daughter's response had been the conventional wisdom at that time. After all, few people make the minimum wage, and there has been much propaganda to the effect that the minimum wage is a job killer—and some on the Right claim that it hurts the US's global competitiveness. Yet, lots of good research shows that increasing the minimum wage is not a job killer. In the main, states that have increased their minimum wage have shown no increase in the unemployment rate compared with geographically contiguous states that did not increase the minimum wage.

Amazing to me at the time, the poll showed that a large majority of Americans were in favor of increasing the minimum wage, including many Republicans. Again, this is a Big Government program, and the numbers indicate that a large majority of Republicans were in favor of it. I suspect that there is an "if you work hard, you ought to make a living wage" attitude among a large majority of Americans.

In a more recent poll (2010), respondents were asked whether or not they were in favor of increasing the minimum wage from $7.25 an hour to $10.00 an hour. Interestingly, 67% of Americans were in favor of increasing it (Delaney 2010). Again, this is a Big Government program, and two-thirds of Americans (likely including a fair number of Republicans) were in favor of the jump to the higher rate.

9. Unemployment Insurance

In a November 2010 poll, 73% of Americans said they wanted to keep the unemployment measure extended to fight the recession (Molyneux 2010). This is an important safety net program for people who lose their jobs. Again, this is a Big Government, essentially liberal program favored by a large majority of Americans.

10. Time-and-a-Half Pay for Overtime

I haven't seen any polls on this subject, but there is little doubt that a large majority of Americans favor it, including many Republicans. Again, it is a Big Government, essentially liberal program.

11. Government Guarantee of up to $250,000 for Bank Deposits

It used to be that when trouble loomed on the horizon, there was often a run on the bank. Depositors tried to get their money out of the bank before the bank was out of money. Some depositors failed to do so and lost their money. To prevent this situation from happening in the future, Franklin Delano Roosevelt signed the Federal Deposit Insurance Corporation (FDIC). The banks pay a fee to finance the program, in which bank deposits are guaranteed up to $250,000. If a bank is in trouble, the FDIC gets it in order and sells it to another, stronger bank. The FDIC has been successful for more than 50 years. I have not seen any polls on the matter, but I am sure that the large majority of Americans are happy with the program, as it protects the safety of their bank deposits, and has essentially eliminated the possibility of "bank runs." Again, it is a Big Government program.

Attitudes Crossing Party Lines

Following are three essentially liberal statements of which a large majority of Americans say they are in favor:

- 64% of Americans say that "labor unions are necessary to protect the working person" (Pew Research Center 2012)
- 65% of Americans say that corporate profits are too high (Pew Research

Center 2007).

- 83% of Americans support stronger laws and regulations to protect the environment (Pew Research Center 2007)

Given the above, it appears that the Republican Party leaders are to the Right of Republican Party members. I also believe that the leaders of the Democratic Party are to the Right of most Democratic voters. I think that the majority of the Democratic base is still liberal, as indicated by their recent revolt concerning President Obama's favorite for Chairman of the Federal Reserve Bank, Larry Summers (Obama didn't end up nominating Summers) (Graham 2013).

Summarizing American Attitudes toward Big Government Programs

The fact that there are nearly 50% more professed conservatives than there are professed liberals might indicate that Americans at least think they are against Big Government programs. However, in practice, most of these same Americans believe they need—and greatly appreciate—the Big Government programs that have been brought to them by liberals, often over the strong objections of the Republicans and Far Right. Even Tea Party adherents, most of whom are considered Far Right, support some of these Big Government social and safety net programs brought to them by the government they say they dislike.

And Americans, I hypothesize, would very likely be in favor of the benefits that most other countries with advanced economies offer by law: a minimum number of paid vacation days, sick days, and maternal/paternal days.

So many Americans talk conservative, and maybe they are, but from a behavioral frame of reference they act like they are very open to Big Government, essentially liberal programs. They may say they don't like Big Government programs, but they approve of most, or all, of those that have been in existence for a while.

Companies Working to Prevent
New Big Government Programs

So why do companies fight so hard (with lobbying and campaign contributions) to prevent government programs that help many Americans. I think there are two major reasons:

1. The CEO and top management want to make as much corporate profits as possible, which leads to a higher stock price and eventually a good reputation and higher compensation for the CEO and top management.

2. These people are wealthy and so they don't need the social and safety net programs that would be of great help to the middle class and other ordinary Americans. Many of the CEOs and top management would much rather have lower taxes than the programs.

It should be remembered that although the government dictates that people get these benefits, private companies often have to pay for some of them.

The CEO of General Electric, Jeffrey Immelt, was appointed head of a commission to improve American exports. What he learned indicates that companies are not as interested in exporting as they say they are. They say they would rather build their warehouses near their (overseas) markets rather than situate them here and export the goods.

If American companies are not as concerned with exporting as expected, why do they work so hard to prevent government programs that would help many Americans? My thinking is cynical. The answer is likely that they simply want to raise corporate profits to be as high as possible, which would increase the stock price.

Part IV

**How to Measure the
New *Stock Price Economy***

CHAPTER 9
**New Economic Measurements for
the New *Stock Price Economy***

CHAPTER 10
**Who Does the Economy Work for Today?
Who Should It Work for?**

CHAPTER 11
**Are the Stock Market Indexes Good Measures
of the Health of the American Economy?**

New Economic Measurements for the New *Stock Price Economy*

From a Business Economy to a *Stock Price Economy*— a Radical Change

A major premise behind this book is that since the US has a new and changed economy, some of the old economic measures are no longer effective in measuring it, and therefore new measurements are necessary. From World War II until the mid- to late-1970s, the US had a Business Economy. Companies were run to be successful for the short, medium, and long term, and workers were valued. Then in the mid- to late-1970s, and especially starting in the very early 1980s, the US economy changed greatly over time to what I call the *Stock Price Economy*, where the key to success was focused on higher short-term corporate profits, resulting in a higher stock price. The medium- and long-term potential were no longer regarded as important by most companies. Workers lost the position they held within the Business Economy as well. Indeed, CEOs learned that workers account for much of the costs of producing a product or service, so the surest way to increase short-term profits and the stock price was to reduce the labor force.

The result has been a lowered standard of living for the bulk of Americans—and Income Inequality, in which the rich (the top 1%) have seen their incomes soar while the middle class and other ordinary Americans (the 99%) have suffered. The pages to come examine how the middle class and other ordinary Americans fared in the Business Economy during the three decades after World War II, followed by how they have done in the *Stock Price Economy* during the most recent three decades.

Accelerating Income Inequality since the Great Recession

Income Inequality has sped up since the Great Recession officially ended. Since that time, the Dow Jones Index has more than doubled—a boon to the wealthy who dominate ownership of stocks, bonds, and other assets—while real wages either remained flat or, for many, decreased.

Essentially, Income Inequality began to completely dominate labor productivity in the 1980s. During the Business Economy, when American workers thrived, they received 91% of labor productivity as wages. During the 1980s, labor productivity increased by 34%, but wages themselves did not increase at all (Mishel, Gould and Bivens 2015).

In a major sense, the middle class is eroding, as is indicated by a *New York Times* series reported August 1, 1999 (the most recent example I saw of this kind of information), titled "The American Middle, Just Getting By," which I quoted in a newsletter I published, *The Middle Class Speaks Up*, more than a decade ago.

The reporter wrote the article 17 years ago (Uchitelle 1999). If it were written today, the situation would be even worse, based on the quantitative data shown in this book. The reporter, Louis Uchitelle of *The New York Times*, wanted to know how the middle class was doing in real life. So he went to Cincinnati, a city with a median income similar to the median income of the US, and interviewed several families with median household incomes.

The reporter's conclusion, shown below, is even truer today than it was 17 years ago: "...the middle-class comforts of an earlier day (post World War II) were accessible to families with just one wage-earner; today middle-class families find they must combine at least two incomes, and often three, in pursuit of a life style that seems always out of reach."

And it is getting worse for average Americans. For example, the Great Recession has hurt average Americans even harder than recessions in the past. The economic state of the average American has fallen sharply during the two years of the recession and still remains much lower than it had been before the Great Recession. On the other hand, since the end of the Great Recession, the incomes of the top 1% have soared.

Workers' Lack of Outrage Possibly Due to Obsolete Economic Measurementss

Income Inequality—and its solution—appear to be an idea whose time has come. However, the problem of Income Inequality has been taking place for more than three decades. Americans are dissatisfied with the economy, but seem to go along with companies doing extraordinarily well and the rich getting richer, while American workers are doing poorly, with the middle class falling apart. It seems to me they should be angrier than they are, considering that Income Inequality has been getting worse for more than three decades. I have a hunch that one reason they are not angrier is because they don't realize how bad they have it from the point of view of actual measurements.

Real wages may mean a great deal to economists and others who have studied them, but I think that most people react viscerally to the nominal wage. If people do not get a cut in nominal salary, they may feel the difference in their lives, but they may not be able to explain why this is so. "Inflation" and "real wages" are powerful but unclear concepts. For example, $1.00 in 1980 would have been worth $2.91 in 2015 (Manuel 2016). In other words, the worth of the dollar fell by 66% (from $2.91 to $1.00) since 1980. If you didn't get raises that made up for this inflation, raises that earned you nearly three times as much as you earned in 1980, you experienced a decrease in purchasing power. I think it is critical to communicate concepts like this in clearer, more intuitive ways than is the case today.

Next, I'd like to show a number of measurement approaches that I believe can do a better job than the ones used today, as the old measurements have not worked properly now for years. Even more important, the newly suggested measurements do a better job of measuring today's economy. Actually this issue of today's economic measurements being inappropriate for today's new economy is not a new concept to me. As mentioned, almost 20 years ago, I published a newsletter called *The Middle Class Speaks Up*, the title of which (for the May 1997 issue) was "How Obsolete Measurements Hide Middle-Class Decline." In this newsletter I covered just this subject—and I've learned quite a bit more about the American economy since then. Below we examine an economic measurement that no longer works in today's economy, followed by several measurements that I believe would work in our current economy.

The Misery Index

The Misery Index used to be an important economic measure, especially since it spoke so clearly to the people. To compute the Misery Index, you simply add the unemployment rate to the inflation rate: clear and easy to compute and understand. If the unemployment rate and inflation rate are higher and/or getting higher, there is more misery. If the unemployment rate and inflation rate are low, the Misery Index is low, and the American people are doing well economically. The last time I heard the Misery Index used was when President Bill Clinton used a low Misery Index to show how well the US economy was doing.

However, it is obvious that the Misery Index no longer works. Following are several of the problems of the Misery Index:

- First, what is unemployment? A lot of Americans are out of a job but not looking because they don't think there are jobs out there. If and when the economy gets stronger, many of these people will search for a job and many will land one. Yet, those who have not looked for a job over the last month because of the shortage of jobs are not considered unemployed. They should be.
- Underemployment should be included in the Misery Index. Those Americans who work part-time, have temporary jobs, or are independent contractors but would like but can't find a full-time, permanent job should be a factor in the Misery Index. Many are in jobs that don't pay a living wage.
- Likely the most important factor not included in this Misery Index is wages—low wages. Some jobs are coming back after the Great Recession, but too often they are lousy (low-paying) jobs. Most of the jobs lost in the Great Recession were high-paying jobs (41%), while most of the jobs gained in the recovery were low-paying jobs (44%). The amount of job compensation should obviously be part of the Misery Index. Low pay can make people feel miserable, and Americans are getting lots of low-paying jobs today.

The economic Misery Index has to be thought through in order to be usable. However, it is important to have a well-thought-through Misery Index in any analysis of the US middle class or US economy.

Economic Measurements that Would Work Better for Measuring the New (Stock Price) Economy:

1. Economic Growth of US by Household Income

The US recovery after the Great Recession has been weak. What is even more eye-opening is that, as mentioned earlier, 95% of all the economic growth in the US for three years after the Great Recession officially ended went to the top 1% of households. In fact, if you go beyond the top 5% of highest income households, the growth becomes less than zero (Cronin 2013). One might say that many in the US have had no growth since the Great Recession. One might even say that many Americans are still in a recession.

All this information is shown in Table 10, which breaks down economic growth (GDP) by household income:

Table 10
Economic Growth (% of GDP) by Household Income

Household Income Percentile	Top 1%	10%	50%	90%
% of Growth of GDP	95%	---	---	---

Monthly, this table would not only show the economic growth of the US, it would also show which people, and to what degree, share in America's prosperity. Chances are that there is enough government data to also do this retroactively. If Americans see month after month that they are not sharing in America's prosperity, many in the middle class and other ordinary Americans might ask for—even demand—their share of US prosperity. When it was recently announced that the US is showing growth, it probably sounded good to most Americans; if it had been announced that the average American was showing no growth—even a loss—many people would realize that they, themselves, were still in a recession.

2. Net Household Income After Fixed Costs of Second Earner

As discussed earlier, Elizabeth Warren and her daughter, Amelia Warren Ty-agi, found that the fixed costs of a second earner entering the workplace are very high. A *net household income statistic* should be computed—reducing total household income by the fixed expenses of the second earner entering the marketplace.

3. Real Wages of the Middle Class, the Top 1%, and Real Corporate Profits Shown in One Table

It is important for Americans to see monthly reports of their own economic status compared to that of the top 1% and corresponding corporate profits. After some time, I think that middle-class Americans and other ordinary Americans might get angry and ask for their share of American prosperity.

If these individuals belonged to a nonprofit, nonpolitical organization targeted at the middle class and those who aspire to join the middle class (recommended and described in a later section), they might have the power to do something about this.

4. Individuals Considered Unemployed—Including Those Who Haven't Searched for Work in a Month

This is another area where the middle class and those who aspire to the middle class will learn that the American economy doesn't function as well as claimed. The unemployed who haven't looked for a job in the past month (because they didn't think any existed) are not considered unemployed. They should be.

5. An Underemployment Table, Broken Down by Part-Time, Temporary, and Individual Contract Workers—All Seeking Full-Time Jobs

In a sense, this could be used as an early warning sign that things are changing. If permanent or part-time or independent contractor jobs are growing—despite the desire of these people to have a full-time job—the nonprofit, nonpolitical middle-class organization we recommend in a later chapter should work hard to communicate this information to Americans, and try to nip a likely recession in the bud.

6. Workers' Wages (High, Medium, or Low)—
for Total Workers

This could be another early warning measurement. If the wages of jobs of middle class and other ordinary workers (the 99%) are not increasing, and there are more and more low-paying jobs, the middle-class organization should work hard to change these dynamics. The idea that Americans can work hard but still not be able to support their families in a middle-class manner is inimical to the American Dream.

It is also inimical to the idea that America is "of the people, by the people, and for the people" (from Abraham Lincoln's Gettysburg Address) (Lincoln 1863). Knowing this and having an organization that works only for the middle class would make it difficult for congressmen and other politicians to ignore these unfair and destructive dynamics.

7. The Percentage of Family-Supporting Jobs

I think this measurement would be eye-opening, and the middle-class organization would go to bat for families led by a person that doesn't hold a family-supporting job. But first, the middle class and other ordinary Americans must be informed of the situation. Those who pay the low wages should be made aware that they are hurting the middle class, and politicians should have this information front and center. I believe that the major loss of the Democrats in the 2014 mid-term elections is largely due to individuals not having living wages despite economic growth in the macro economy. It is said that all politics is local. Let me go further. What is also critical is how well individuals are doing, not only the overall economy.

We currently use a measure of poverty. I don't see why a measure of a family-supporting wage cannot be developed as well.

8. Total Tax Rate Broken Down by Household Income

Usually, the tax data we see includes only the federal income tax, which accounts for only 25.5% of all taxes collected in the US—and the wealthy (top 1%) pay 38% of all the federal income tax (2011 figures) (US Government Revenue 2011). Yet, when you consider all (total) taxes, and include federal payroll taxes

(Social Security and Medicare), and state and local taxes, the wealthy (top 1%) don't pay that much more of their income in taxes than the median/average American.

Also, when we consider low-income Americans only (the bottom 40%), they pay a significant total tax rate on their incomes—19.3%, not zero, as is claimed by many on the Right, including Mitt Romney. Indeed, I am sure there are years when Romney paid an even lower total tax rate than 19.3%, especially if the state in which he resided didn't have a state tax or had a very low state tax. It is an accounting trick to count only federal income tax, of which the wealthy (top 1%) pay a significant amount.

9. Percentage of Productivity Going to Wages versus Corporate Profits

As mentioned earlier, in the three decades following World War II, the percentage of productivity that went to worker wages was 91%. In the most recent three decades, however, real wages increased by only 10%, which means that only 13% of productivity went to workers in wages. Americans won't like the idea if they realize that if they received the same percentage of productivity they received in the three decades after World War II, the average household would have received a raise of $36,600 a year (78% of $47,000). By siphoning off the share of labor productivity that used to go to real wages, employers are sharply reducing real wages while sharply increasing corporate profits and stock prices.

Communicating This Information

How to communicate this information to the American people? It would take a long, long time to convince the Census Bureau or the Bureau of Economic Analysis (BEA) to do so. However, I suggest that the new data be computed monthly and distributed to the media by the nonprofit, nonpolitical economic organization for the middle class that I recommend be established. Sending this information monthly to the media would be an effective approach, as the media could easily communicate it to the American people. I think that some of the new criteria would be exciting to many Americans, including some economists. There's probably enough data to get some of the information retroactively, which should be eye-opening.

Chapter 10

Who Does the Economy Work for Today? Who Should It Work for?

Consider the question: In whose interests does the economy function today? It is obviously the wealthy (top 1% in household income). Some examples:

- There is huge Income Inequality. In 1980, the wealthy (top 1% of households) had an income that was 10 times the income of the median household. By 2006, 26 years later, the top 1% had an average income that was 29 times the median household (Congressional Budget Office 2009). In less than three decades, Income Inequality had tripled.
- The Income Inequality has been getting worse and worse, with the wealthy (top 1%) getting close to 95% of the growth in the first three years after the Great Recession. Millions of Americans are really still in a recession.
- Earlier, we discussed 10 tax myths. In every case, the myth works in favor of the top 1% or 2%.

It is useful to explore what Abraham Lincoln had to say about who the economy should benefit. It makes simple common sense in a country that is supposed to be class-less. As mentioned earlier, probably Abraham Lincoln's most famous line, from the Gettysburg Address, was that the US was "of the people, by the people and for the people." Lincoln wasn't talking about the top 1%. He was saying that America should be for 100% of the people.

Aside from the aspect of fairness, it would appear that 90% or more of the population not prospering is bad for the economy. In the three decades after World War II, not only did median real wages increase every one of the 26 years from 1947 to 1973, but the five quintiles (in 20% chunks) increased their income at about the same rate. There was Income Equality. The economy was most often successful, and the US built the largest middle class in the history of the world. In short, Income Equality seems to correspond with a successful economy for Americans.

Other evidence:

- In 1993, President Bill Clinton increased the tax on the wealthy, increasing the marginal federal income tax rate (paid by the wealthy) from 31% to 39.6% (by 27.7%). The Republicans predicted this would be followed by a deep recession. Instead, it was followed by a very long recovery, and more than 22 million net new jobs were developed during the eight years of the Clinton administration (Waldman 2014).
- On the other hand, President George W. Bush reduced the taxes paid essentially by the wealthy: the federal income tax, the capital gains tax, the dividend tax, and the estate tax. This was followed by the weakest recovery since the Great Depression, which was followed in turn by the financial disaster in 2008, leading to the Great Recession, which we are still attempting to recover from five years later.

In summary, Income Inequality is not only unfair, it is bad economics.

Finally, a research study was recently conducted by the Federal Reserve Bank which throws light on the question of what happens with the increased incomes of the wealthy (the millionaires). The results were reported in the *New York Post* on November 2, 2014 (Bresiger 2014):

- Yes, the rich are getting richer, but many of them shop at Walmart, clip coupons, and don't drive a Lexus.
- Having short arms and deep pockets is the main driver that allows the one-percenter to be an accumulator of wealth, according to the Atlanta-based American Affluence Center.

The 99 percenter has to spend the money he or she gets much more quickly. The wealthy do not. Again, in our demand-side economy, Income Inequality, with the incomes of the 1% soaring and the 99% lagging, is not only lacking in morality, it is bad economics.

Chapter 11

Are the Stock Market Indexes Good Measures of the Health of the American Economy?

This is a very short chapter, but an important one. Whenever the question is asked about the state of the economy, a great deal of stress is laid upon the soaring stock market, as rising stock prices have always been considered a major plus for the economy. This was appropriate during the Business Economy, when the stock market was generally an accurate reflection of the economy.

However, this is no longer the case since the US switched to the *Stock Price Economy*. Not only is the stock price seen as an end in itself, it is seen as the main objective. Also, in the *Stock Price Economy*, a booming stock market can actually hurt the economy in the following major ways:

- First, CEOs realize that labor costs account for much of the total cost of producing a product or service. So, they have significantly lowered labor costs. Not only does this hurt workers but it denies workers and their families the necessary funds to fulfill their wants and needs. In a major sense, companies are "starving their customers." This results in lower sales and a weak economy.

- Second, in a *Stock Price Economy*, it means that companies are not purchasing enough capital goods. The result may be higher short-term corporate profits and stock prices, but it will be an obstacle to true (top-line sales) growth of companies, and eventually, to the true growth of the overall economy.

- In the *Stock Price Economy*, a booming stock market can lead to a weak overall economy. Companies do well on the bottom line (corporate profits), but poorly on the top line (sales). In this book, a CEO is quoted as saying that his company had learned how to make money (corporate profits) in an economy that increased at a very weak 1% per year. This may be great for the company's short-term stock price, but it is terrible for workers and the overall economy.

In a Business Economy, a soaring stock market usually means that the economy is doing very well. In the *Stock Price Economy*, on the other hand, it can easily mean that workers are suffering, and the overall economy is as well.

Part V

**How the American People
Are Misled about
Their Economic Situation**

CHAPTER 12
Political and Economic Terms That Lie

CHAPTER 13
"Flag-Waving" versus "Economic" Patriotism

Chapter 12

Political and Economic Terms That Lie

I find it amazing how clever the Right Wing is at finding terms that are effective in marketing their ideas but are false, whereas the Democrats seem to be inept both at countering them and marketing their own (often true) claims. Most often, the Right demonizes the Democratic position, but sometimes they just select terms or phrases that make their points sound more promising than they really are.

Discussed in the following pages are nine cases of demonization and five of the terms that enhance their positions. Sometimes the effective, false terms and concepts are used in advertising and sometimes in "talking points" (often both), where it seems that Right Wing congressmen, media, etc. use the same terms to criticize the Democratic position, making it likely that the claims and terms came from a single source.

Other than in elections, where Democrats have finally realized that in order to win, you must fight fire with fire—by adopting a negative spin—the Democrats do a poor job in making important accusations about the Republican positions, even if the accusations are true and would be compelling to many Americans. It is as if the Democrats do a good job during elections, at least in presidential election years, and then stop using the approach until the next election, whereas the Republicans conduct a four-year (continuous) campaign, often using false, but effective, accusations against the Democrats.

This analysis is used to show that the middle-class organization I recommend later in this book should have a permanent "War Room" to quickly rebut false accusations of the opposition, and to develop tough strategies to use in winning the public debate on public policy issues.

False but Effective Terms Used by the Right to Demonize Democratic Positions

1. The Death Tax

The Right has demonized the 100-year-old estate tax as a "death tax," as if it were a double whammy—not only does a person die, but his or her estate is then taxed (Green 2001). Actually the estate tax is not a death tax. It is a wealth tax that is determined after death, which is the practical time to handle it because that is when the size of the estate can best be established.

Several important people have defended the estate tax. Both Theodore and Franklin Delano Roosevelt saw it as a case of morality and as good for democracy. Basically, they saw it as leveling the playing field, as should be the case in a democracy. Even Adam Smith, essentially the father of economics and capitalism, said that he found it difficult to defend money left by the deceased to heirs unless an heir needed the money for a long-term problem. Teddy Roosevelt felt that if left a great deal of money, too many people would not live admirable lives.

As a result of the Right's demonization, the estate tax has been cut sharply—Romney even said he was in favor of repealing the estate tax. The Democrats have essentially allowed the Republicans to get away with this false "death tax" vilification.

2. Death Panels

When the Affordable Care Act (ObamaCare) was introduced, the Right accused of it of using "death panels" in which a panel of people would decide when life should end. A Republican senator even said (likely jocularly) that they were trying to kill grandma. But even opponents of the measure had to admit this charge wasn't true, so they let up on the claim. However, as often happens, "death panels" are still brought up at times as a throwaway argument, without any evidence.

3. The Individual Mandate

The major criticism by the opponents of the Affordable Care Act is the Individual Mandate. In this mandate, if someone without a healthcare policy from a job or other place can afford to buy one but doesn't, he or she must pay a fine. This was instituted because otherwise many Americans in good health would not apply for a healthcare policy until they got sick, at which time they would not be refused healthcare insurance because of a pre-existing condition. This would make for a sicker pool of early buyers that would make healthcare insurance more expensive overall.

Yet, the backers of the Affordable Care Act have allowed the opponents to get away with this demonization. The Act's opponents say that it takes away liberty and freedom from Americans. It should have been (and still can be) relatively easy to effectively counter this demonization. Following are four approaches that could deal effectively with this demonization of the Individual Mandate:

- First, the Individual Mandate idea was developed by a Right Wing Conservative think tank and used by the Republicans in the early 1990s to combat President Bill Clinton's attempt at universal healthcare (Roy 2012). At that time, the Republicans said it was a matter of individual responsibility for people to get their own healthcare insurance (the Individual Mandate).
- It seems obvious that the Republicans are against the Individual Mandate just because it was offered by Obama and the Democrats. After all, the Republicans were in favor of the Individual Mandate when it was offered by the Republicans.
- Americans are not against mandates per se. A very large majority of Americans (82%) are in favor of a mandate for insurance companies to offer healthcare insurance to those with pre-existing conditions, and a very large majority of Americans (72%) are in favor of a mandate requiring companies with more than 50 employees to offer healthcare to all their full-time employees (ObamaCare Facts 2012). Yet the backers of the Affordable Care Act have allowed their opponents to get away with the claim that Americans are against mandates in general, and the Individual Mandate in particular.

• The Individual Mandate keeps healthcare costs down for the majority of Americans. Without it, healthy Americans are less likely to purchase health-care insurance, resulting in a sicker pool of Americans, which would lead to a higher cost for a healthcare policy for the majority of Americans.

However, the backers of the Affordable Care Act have essentially allowed their opponents thus far to get away with the demonization of the Individual Mandate concept—and what they call "ObamaCare."

4. Regulations

To many on the Right, all regulations are negative. What short memories these people have. The Great Recession, from which many people are still trying to extricate themselves, was to a major degree caused by a good deal of deregu-lation. The investment banks and big banks were allowed to do significantly more "betting"—and risk-taking—using money deposited by Americans and guaranteed by the government.

Without good regulation, there isn't the level playing field necessary for a well-functioning free market for the banking sector. As we learned, this can easily lead to financial disaster and the need for huge sums of government money to bail out the big banks.

On the other hand, good regulation can prevent a financial disaster. The Glass-Steagall Act, for example, passed during the FDR administration, pre-vented banks from using any deposits guaranteed by the government for their own investment banking purposes. This helped prevent the occurrence of fi-nancial disaster for more than 70 years since it was passed in 1933, until the Glass-Steagall law and other bank regulations were repealed during the Bill Clinton administration (Long 2015).

Yet, the Right is allowed to too easily use the argument that "America has big financial problems because there is too much regulation." The Democrats should remind Americans that the bailouts and the Great Recession, whose effects they are still feeling, were largely caused by too little regulation and that too little regulation is one of the major causes of middle-class erosion.

5. Government

The Right Wingers believe that aside from fighting wars, the "government" can't do anything well. Ronald Reagan put it this way: "Government is not the solution to our problem; government is the problem" (The Heritage Foundation 1981). The "government" has been so demonized that even the Democratic president, Bill Clinton, felt it important enough to say: "The era of big government is over" (Clinton 1996).

Yet the government has developed many programs that are critical to the lives of Americans—and that the private sector wouldn't/couldn't develop—Social Security, Medicare, Medicaid, FHA/Veteran's mortgages, Securities Exchange Commission (SEC), FDIC guarantee of private bank deposits up to $250,000, disability insurance, flood insurance, the minimum wage, the Tennessee Valley Administration, the cross-country railroad system, the cross-country US road system, Boulder Dam, etc. Often, the Republicans opposed these programs at first, and even today, would like to cut or even repeal some of them—though the large majority of Americans remain strongly in favor of them.

The Democrats have done little to act upon this criticism of too much "government." In fact, the very opposite—more government—would probably be very helpful. Americans need to be reminded that the bank bailouts and the Great Recession, whose effects they are still smarting from, were largely caused by insufficient government regulation. They also need to be reminded that the government regulations put into effect during and after the Great Depression worked well for 60–70 years—until the regulations were repealed. Also, Jeffrey Immelt, CEO of GE, was quoted as saying that the government has done much for the US, and was specific about how the government is responsible for most of the developments in the airline and healthcare industries (CBS News 2011).

William Lazonick, in his article "Nine Government investments that made us an Industrial Economic Leader," named nine major industries in which the government played the key role in making the US government a leader in the industry (Lazonick 2011):

1. Railroads
2. Universities
3. Agriculture
4. Aircraft
5. Jet engines
6. College-educated labor force
7. Interstate highway source
8. Computers and the Internet
9. Life sciences

Jeffrey Immelt is correct in his rebuttal of the current "put down" (including by President Reagan and the Right Wing) that the government cannot do anything right—that only entrepreneurs and the free market can do it right (CBS News 2011). If one studies the industries listed above, it is obvious that as the industry began, none seemed ready to be economically feasible until the government brought the industry to the stage where private industry could see its way to make profits in the industry. The government was necessary to use, and pay for, R&D that would bring an industry to the point where the private sector thought it would make money.

The government is necessary for much more than picking winners and losers. If the government is read out of the equation, the US would have been left out of many important industries, because at the start, many industries are not ready to make money, and the government is needed to bring the industries to the point where the private sector can take over. And, in some areas, the private sector never wants to fully take over. In any case, government R&D is very useful to many private sector industries.

Can you imagine the US being a significant industrial power without the above industries?

6. Socialism

It often seems as if everything that is or would be helpful to the mainstream of the American people is labeled as "socialism." If you ask Right Wingers if Social Security, Medicare, the minimum wage, or unemployment insurance are forms of socialism, the answer for all would probably be "yes."

I doubt that these programs could be passed today, even though it has turned out that the American people appreciate, even love, many of these programs. I think that the term "socialism" is often used interchangeably with "government" by the opponents of these programs.

It is ironic that countries like Germany, which has many more of these big government, essentially liberal programs that help workers and other ordinary people than the US does, seems more successful at capitalism than we are. Germany exports twice as much to the US as the US exports to Germany (Travisa 2016). And Germany has a very large trade surplus with the US and the world. The US, on the other hand, exports only half as much to Germany as Germany exports to the US, and the US has the largest trade deficit, by far, in the world.

Yet, the fact that the US runs a trade deficit with many of the countries that offer excellent social and safety net programs than the US indicates that this lack of government action (called "socialism" by its opponents) isn't strengthening US capitalism in the global economy.

7. "Socialized Medicine"

The phrase "socialized medicine" was developed about 65 years ago by a public relations firm in order to help the American Medical Association (AMA) defeat an attempt by President Harry Truman to institute a universal healthcare system in the US, and has been used ever since for the same purpose—to defeat any attempt at universal healthcare (Palmer 1999). Truman said that the US was spending only 4% of GDP on healthcare, and could afford to spend more. His universal healthcare bill was defeated, so today 33 million Americans are uninsured, which causes thousands of Americans to die, according to an estimate by research from Harvard, and hundreds of thousands, perhaps even millions of Americans have their illness worsened because they put off healthcare because of cost (Cecere 2009). The US now spends 17% to 18% of its GDP on healthcare and twice as much per capita on healthcare as the average advanced country with a universal healthcare system, yet often has poorer outcomes (The Commonwealth Fund 2015). The US made a very wrong call on the Truman universal healthcare bill.

"Government-run healthcare," as opponents call it, is not even an accurate accusation. In most countries with a universal healthcare system, although the government makes sure everybody is covered, the healthcare system is run privately by doctors and the other healthcare providers, just as it is in the US. Ironically, the private-sector Health Maintenance Organizations (HMOs) in the US get more involved in the healthcare system than is the case in countries with universal healthcare systems. Even in the US, the Medicare system (run by the government) gets much less involved in the doctor-patient relationship than is the case with the privately-owned and run HMOs.

As mentioned earlier, I think that denying people healthcare insurance is "cruel and unusual punishment." It is cruel because it leads to the deaths of thousands of people a year, and likely hundreds of thousands or even millions of people get sicker because they put off healthcare due to cost—until they are eligible for Medicare. It is unusual because the US is the only advanced country in the world without a universal healthcare system (where everyone living in the country is covered), and there are many non-advanced countries that also have universal healthcare systems.

8. Liberal

This term has been so demonized that even those who are liberals tend to use the term "progressive" or the "progressive movement" to describe their political attitudes. As can be seen in Table 11 (Saad 2010), a June 2010 Gallup poll showed that most Americans (54%) say they are unsure whether the term "progressive" describes their views, 31% say that it does not describe their views, and only 12% say that it does describe their views:

Table 11
Does "Progressive" Describe Your Political View?

	Describes	Does Not Describe	Unsure
National View	12%	31%	54%
Democrats	20%	22%	57%
Independent	10%	29%	61%
Republican	7%	49%	43%

Table 11 shows that even among Democrats, "progressive" does not describe their views (22% to 20%). The same is true among Independents, except by a much wider margin (29% to 10%). By an even wider margin, Republicans say it does not describe their views (49% to 7%).

Among those who say that "progressive" does describe their views, the term "does not describe their views" wins over "describes their views"—and by 31% to 12%, a two-and-a-half to one margin.

It is just my hunch, but I think that the reason the term "progressive" in politics is a negative is that it means "very Left Wing" to many Americans (including me.) I know that when Theodore Roosevelt ran on the third party, he called it the "Progressive Party." However, in more recent years "Progressive" is part of the name of third parties and organizations that tend to be very Left Wing.

One possibility is to go back to using the term "liberal." Americans could be reminded that the programs that make their lives better were instituted by liberals over the sharp criticism of many Republicans who fought against them before they were instituted—and that many on the Right are still trying to cut or even repeal some of these programs even now. For example, it is the Right that would like to cut the "entitlements," Social Security, and Medicare, even though most Republicans (even most Tea Party adherents) are in favor of maintaining them as is.

Maybe times are changing. Democratic entrance and exit polls in the past eight years (three elections) show a sharp increase in the percentage who said they were liberals.

9. Unions

Although many American workers see themselves as essentially helpless on the job and badly in need of assistance in negotiating rights, quite a few Americans say they are against unions. The attitude of Americans towards unions is paradoxical. Although American opinions are very mixed in terms of favorability, a large majority say that unions are necessary. For example, a *Washington Post*/ABC News poll in March 2011 asked "Do you think workers in this country should or should not have a right to form unions to negotiate with employers on issues like their working conditions, pay, benefits, and pensions?"

No fewer than 81% said they should, compared with only 18% who said they should not. There are several other polls as well where the large majorities (more than 60%) think that workers should hold the right to form unions (Washington Post/ABC News 2011).

Research shows that many people think unions would benefit workers, but not companies or trade—demonstrating, I believe, that Right Wing propaganda demonizing unions has taken its toll.

Deep down, however, I think that a large majority of Americans know they need a body to represent them in negotiating for pay, benefits, working conditions, etc., and I believe a good advertising and promotion campaign could help make unions strong again. One major problem the union's face conceptually in the US is that Americans think that unions are a thing of the past and will continue to lose power.

However, I have confidence that a good advertising and public relations campaign for unions could make them much more popular and relevant to Americans. The campaign would have to communicate that the new unions would be different from the old, essentially "not like your grandfather's union." The campaign should portray the union (or works council) to look and sound like a twenty-first-century institution as opposed to what has been seen in outdated newsreels and movies—no more union leaders smoking fat cigars.

Interestingly, Volkswagen instituted a works council even though the workers were bamboozled by the politicians into voting against it. I guess the thinking on the part of Volkswagen was that works councils work well in Germany, so why not in the US? Perhaps the thinking on the part of the American politicians was "you can't trust unions."

A lot of thinking—and probably research—has to be done on this issue by the unions. Germany has works councils, comprised of workers in companies. Indeed, by law, large companies must have a worker on the Board of Directors.

Something else to note: In Germany, there is much less of an adversarial relationship between employers and workers than in the US. Both groups are aware that in order for each to succeed, the company must thrive overall. Perhaps the existence of works councils are a factor in this less adversarial approach. I believe this approach might be good for America, that it may have both management and workers thinking and working hard for the company. Could this approach work in America? I believe there are some employers who would be willing to attempt it. I think this approach might help right the Income Inequality problem and even make "true growth" as, or more, important than short-term profits, and would motivate CEOs to think longer term than they do today.

I believe that a well-funded, smart advertising and public relations program would be successful and lead to a sharp increase in the pressure from the American people to push for unionism in the private sector. Today, nobody is representing over 90% of workers in the private sector and, again, many of these workers feel helpless on the job—in short, they feel they are being exploited.

Political Terms That Make Negative Concepts Sound Positive

Most of the political terms that lie are used by the Right to disparage their opponents and their views. However, some of the "lies" attempt to make the words or concepts favored by the Right seem more positive than they really are.

1. The Job Creators

When the idea is broached of increasing the taxes of the wealthy, the Right Wing/Tea Party warns that it would be a job killer, because the wealthy are the job creators. This is just an assertion on their part, without showing any concrete evidence.

Actually, I think this assertion is wrong. In 1993, as mentioned earlier, the Bill Clinton administration financial plan sharply increased the marginal federal income tax rate (paid heavily by the wealthy) from 31% to 39.6%, an increase of 27.7%. Again, the Republicans claimed there would be a deep recession because the job creators were being heavily taxed. Instead, there was a very long economic expansion, with the development of 22+ million net new jobs in Bill Clinton's eight-year administration.

On the other hand, as also mentioned earlier, when George W. Bush became president, his financial plan decreased the marginal federal income tax rate from 39.6% to 35%, reduced the long-range capital gains rate tax, and sharply reduced the dividend tax rate from the marginal federal income tax rate (39.6%) to 15%. He also significantly lowered the estate tax. All these taxes are paid essentially by the rich (top 1%).

What were the results of these cuts? The Bush tax cuts led to the weakest economic expansion since World War II, followed by the financial disaster on Wall Street. That was followed by the Great Recession from which the US is still attempting to recover.

I believe that the wealthy are not the job creators—rather, that average Americans (the middle class, those who aspire to the middle class, and other ordinary Americans—the 99%) are the true job creators. It's my belief that buying in our society begins with ordinary people, and to do that people have to be able to afford it—it's the demand side that's critical, not the supply side. It is no coincidence that the American economy today has a demand problem. Unemployment and underemployment were kept high as long as possible, while wages were kept low. American business essentially starved its customers.

I believe that when average Americans make enough money from their jobs and are purchasing goods, employers produce more goods and services. Employers only make more products and services when people are buying (demand-side). That tells them that their wares are needed and will be purchased.

The reverse is not true. If companies simply go ahead and make more products and services (supply-side), Americans will not necessarily buy them. Supply-side economics—which states that just producing products will lead to purchase—most often doesn't really work in the American marketplace, or anyplace, especially in countries with advanced economies. If people don't earn enough money from their jobs, they don't buy as much as when they are paid well for their work.

Yet, the Right continues to warn about increasing taxes on the wealthy, who they claim are the "job creators." They are not. Interestingly, Americans, in a poll, are emphatic that they are not against taxing the rich more. Far more Americans believe that the primary way to balance the budget is to increase taxes on the rich (61%) rather than think the entitlement programs Medicare (4%) and Social Security (3%) should be cut. Yet, reducing the entitlement programs is on the table, while taxing the rich more is not. Clearly, the American people are not being heard.

2. Supply-Side Economics

The modern supply-side economic theory was given new life by Arthur Laffer in the early 1980s, at the beginning of the Reagan administration. It is often described as the Laffer Curve (The Laffer Center 2014). Laffer explains that the more money that is taken from the wealthy, the less intensely they will work.

Conversely, the less revenue (e.g., taxes) that is received from them, the more intensely they will work and the more they will produce. The result will be that more tax will be received by the government. Also, because the wealthy work hard and ostensibly make more money, a lower tax rate can actually result in more money collected by the government in the end.

This approach didn't work for either President Ronald Reagan or President George W. Bush. The sharp cut in taxes during the Reagan administration led to huge deficits, so much so that taxes had to be increased several times, and the tax cuts by President George W. Bush also led to the huge deficits still faced by the US. Actually, the large tax cuts by President George W. Bush turned a budget surplus into a very large budget deficit.

Interestingly, many who used the concept of supply-side economics did not really believe in it. In an interview in *The Atlantic* magazine, David Stockman, the first budget director for Reagan and the lead man on Reagan's first financial plan, admitted that the term "supply-side economics" was a ploy (Greider 1981). He admitted that it is really just the old Republican "trickle-down" economics, but it's hard to sell "trickle-down" to the people. The real objective of the tax cut, Stockman said, was always to sharply reduce the marginal rate of the federal income tax paid by the wealthy. They greatly succeeded at this, eventually reducing the marginal federal income tax rate (paid by the wealthy) from 70% to 28%.

Before the "supply-side" ploy, the Republicans used the term "capital appreciation" to communicate falsely that tax decreases for the wealthy were critical. "Capital appreciation" is also a supply-side concept. Basically, I think that the wealthy want to lower taxes because they have no need for the social or safety net programs those taxes usually pay for.

Actually, I do think that supply-side economics works when the tax rate is prohibitive. For example, when John F. Kennedy reduced the marginal federal income tax rate from 91% to 70%, it helped the economy. The wealthy tended to stop "hiding" their money in tax avoidance schemes. However, supply-side economics has caused major problems with the economy when Reagan reduced the tax rate from 70% to 50%, and certainly when he reduced it from 50% to 28%.

3. American Exceptionalism

This is a major factor in the poor performance of the US in a number of areas. As mentioned earlier, "America has the greatest healthcare system in the world" rolls so easily off the tongue. However, it is not true. On the other hand, business doesn't believe in American exceptionalism. When an American company has a problem with a product or service, it compares them with those of a world-class company. For example, when Xerox was having a great deal of trouble with its copiers, it looked to the Japanese copier companies, the most successful in the world.

4. Free Market versus Laissez Faire

I don't think there has been a conscious effort to fool Americans here. However, I do think that this difference between the free market and laissez faire is critical to the US economy, and is a basic reason for some of its major problems.

I remember when President Reagan said that he would solve the major Savings & Loan Bank problem by turning the free market loose on it. He didn't succeed because the Savings & Loan Banks were given laissez faire (Reagan deregulated them), but did not set up a free market (Krugman 2009).

A great many S&Ls had to close, and hundreds of billions of dollars were lost. Lots of the executives treated the money in the S&L banks as if it were their own, and hundreds of S&L executives went to jail. Reagan had mistaken "laissez faire" for the "free market." Essentially, Reagan had removed the regulations from the S&Ls and allowed the executives to do as they liked with the money deposited in the S&Ls.

One way or another, much of the money ended up in the pockets of the S&L executives. This may be laissez faire, but it certainly is not a free market. The terms "free market" and "laissez faire" have very different meanings, yet many Americans use them interchangeably. Actually, programs that have laissez faire but are not a free market are responsible for many problems in the US economy. For example, in the 1990s and the early 2000s, big banks and Wall Street had most of their regulations removed, which allowed the investment functions of banks to do what they wanted. This was laissez faire, but it was by no means a true free market. Many investment banks played their customers for "suckers," with products that customers, and sometimes even the CEOs of the banks, did not even understand, like "derivatives." The result was the financial disaster in 2008, followed by the Great Recession.

In a true free market, whether or not there is regulation, both sides in the transaction must have similar information and negotiate in their own self-interest. In a major sense, when I was in business, it was a free market. The client had three bids on a project. If I didn't give a fair price, I didn't get the project, and if I didn't do a quality job, I wouldn't get any other jobs from the client. In my experience, the free market works extremely well—but only if it is a true free market.

Six years after the new regulations bill (Dodd-Frank) was passed, many of the new rules have not yet been imposed. The lobbyist problem must be solved, but that is the subject of another book.

Karl Rove's Rule on Winning Elections

I disagree with Karl Rove on practically all issues. However, I agree with him on perhaps his key strategic rule: Politics is won on the offensive and lost on the defensive. The Republicans win on some issues they have no right winning, and they do it by going on the offensive—very often by spewing untruths. The Democrats, on the other hand, lose on issues they should easily win, because they too often use a defensive approach between elections, and very often don't do that well.

As I learned during many years of marketing research, words matter a lot. The Republicans realize this, and the Democrats don't seem to pay enough attention to this between elections. This is why the Republicans win public debates on issues that should be won by Democrats.

I remember President Bill Clinton saying that "politics is a contact sport" (Harris 2010). It is, and the Democrats should learn to get on the offensive in a continuous manner between elections. It will also help them win elections.

The major problem here is that while the Democrats have learned that it is critical to "fight fire with fire" during elections, they turn down the intensity of these dynamics when the election is over, whereas the Republicans lead an ongoing four-year campaign, enabling them to win debates on public issues that could easily be won by the Democrats if they went on the attack. In President Bill Clinton's first campaign, for example, they created a "War Room," in which they quickly countered Republican falsehoods and developed strategies that he used to win the election. The "War Room" was even made into a very popular documentary.

Chapter 13

"Flag-Waving" versus "Economic" Patriotism

Two Kinds of Patriotism

Usually a single word or term is used for this concept: patriotism. However, this chapter shows that two terms should be used: "flag-waving" patriotism and "economic" patriotism.

Interestingly, the American presidents who have screamed "patriotism" the loudest have tended to be "flag-waving" patriots but not "economic" patriots. But there have been presidents who were both. These presidents have tended not to scream "patriotism" quite so loudly.

Reagan and Bush: "Flag-Waving" Patriots, Not "Economic" Patriots

President Reagan saw himself as a great patriot. He spoke about America as "a house on a hill," and was loved by most Americans for saying it. President George W. Bush was also known as a patriot—he even called one of his bills the Patriot Act, as if you weren't a patriot if you voted against it.

However, in both the Reagan and Bush presidencies, the wealthy thrived while the middle class and other ordinary Americans did not. Over the more than three decades since Ronald Reagan became president, the American middle class has badly eroded, and this erosion is speeding up. Both Reagan and Bush sharply cut the taxes of the rich (especially Reagan, who cut the marginal income tax rate from 70% to 28%) but gave the middle class and other ordinary Americans little—especially because they pay mainly entitlement taxes (Social Security and Medicare), and state and local taxes.

Reagan-Bush Tax Cuts:

Three points should be noted about the Reagan and Bush tax cuts::

- The taxes that were cut most were the ones that the wealthy (top 1%) pay most heavily: the federal income tax and the financial taxes—the capital gains tax, the dividend tax, and the estate tax.
- The federal income tax accounts for only 25.5% of all the taxes collected in the US (US Government Revenue 2011). The federal payroll taxes (Social Security and Medicare), state taxes, and local taxes—the taxes which average Americans pay heavily—account for about three-quarters of the total taxes collected in the US, and these taxes have not been cut (other than a temporary cut, which has already ended, in the payroll taxes due to the recent Great Recession).
- Considering the above, when the Republicans say that 47% of Americans pay no tax, it is true that they may pay no federal income tax, but they pay heavy federal payroll taxes, state taxes, and local taxes. Their actions on financial matters show that Ronald Reagan and George W. Bush were primarily interested in helping the wealthy. Consequently, Reagan and Bush were "flag-waving" patriots but not "economic" patriots, certainly not for the middle class and other ordinary Americans.

Post-World-War-II Democratic Presidents: Both "Economic" and "Flag-Waving" Patriots

By contrast, the four essentially liberal Democratic presidents—FDR, Harry Truman, John F. Kennedy, and Lyndon B. Johnson—were part of an economic "run" from post-World War II to 1968. As mentioned earlier, the real wages (controlling for inflation) of US workers from 1947 to 1973 increased every year, for a total 75% increase in real wages. The result was the development of the largest middle class in the history of the world.

Franklin Delano Roosevelt

FDR was the president who did most to grow the middle class and help other ordinary Americans. He was mainly responsible for Social Security (probably the most successful US program in American history), Unemployment Insurance, Disability Insurance, the very successful GI Bill of Rights after World War II, the Federal Housing Administration (FHA) and Veteran's mortgages, the SEC and the Glass-Steagall Act (which helped prevent a new Wall Street financial disaster for 70 years until it was repealed), the Tennessee Valley Authority (aka the TVA, which provided electricity to millions of Americans without electricity), the minimum wage, and the Wagner Act (which made unionization available if a majority of a company's workers voted for it).

In my view, the Wagner Act was the factor most responsible for the growth of the middle class because it made labor unions much easier to vote in. The union represented the worker, who isn't really represented in the private sector today—a major cause of our current Income Inequality. Roosevelt also brought hope to Americans, who had fallen into a terrible state of despair. Most importantly, he led to the passage of a large amount of social and safety net legislation, many of which remain today—and are now favored by a very large majority of Americans.

Harry Truman

Truman fought a defensive fight for FDR's liberal government programs. Truman's advisors recommended that he send to Congress a more conservative program, but Truman refused. He sent a liberal program to Congress, including a universal healthcare bill. Congress didn't pass his program, but Truman at least defended FDR's programs and won reelection by running against the "Do-Nothing Congress" (Truman 1948).

John Fitzgerald Kennedy and Lyndon Baines Johnson

(LBJ passed several bills introduced by JFK, so the two are placed together.) Under pressure, Congress passed quite a few bills, but two in particular really helped the middle class and other senior Americans: Medicare and Medicaid. Medicare was for all seniors 65 and older, and Medicaid was intended for the poor, but much—perhaps most—of Medicaid money is spent on long-term care for seniors.

Before Medicare, about half of seniors did not have healthcare insurance, as healthcare insurance for seniors is often very expensive. The rates are higher for older people because older people are most likely to get sick—even very sick, much more likely than the young. As the poor very often cannot afford healthcare insurance, Medicaid is obviously very important to them as well.

Medicare is very important to the finances of seniors overall. As mentioned, many seniors face illness, and healthcare is extraordinarily expensive if you don't have insurance. Even with the help of Medicare, seniors spend a lot on healthcare, but without it, the cost would be so prohibitive that many seniors with a serious illness couldn't afford treatment at all.

As a program, Medicare has financial problems that need to be solved, but I believe that this is mainly due to the explosion of healthcare costs. Regardless, there is no question that Americans support Medicare.

All other countries with advanced economies (and many non-advanced economies) have universal healthcare. These countries cover everyone with healthcare insurance, very often with positive outcomes. Some of these countries with universal healthcare have better outcomes than US healthcare and at a much lower cost per capita. The countries with universal healthcare view healthcare as a right of every citizen, and a responsibility of government to those citizens. They believe that if you get sick, you have a right to be treated. This is not the case in the US.

Post-World War II Republican Presidents: Upholding Taxes, Safety Net, and Social Programs

Dwight Eisenhower: Maintaining Most of the New Deal and Its Tax Ways

The single Republican president during this 26-year period after World War II, Dwight Eisenhower, didn't try to cut taxes or end the New Deal programs. Eisenhower was a small-government Republican, but he didn't try to repeal the liberal safety-net and social programs developed by the Democratic presidents who preceded him. Following is a segment of a letter from Dwight Eisenhower to his brother, Milton Eisenhower, then president of Columbia University (Eisenhower 1954):

"Should any political party attempt to abolish social security, unemployment insurance, and eliminate labor laws and farm programs, you wouldn't hear of that party again in our political history. There is a tiny splinter group, of course, that believes that you can do these things. Among them are a few

Texas oil millionaires, and an occasional politician or businessman from other areas. Their number is negligible and they are stupid."

Eisenhower was not a good prognosticator. The fringe group of Republicans—"some millionaires and billionaires"—was able to push the essentially moderate Republican Party (to which Eisenhower belonged) into becoming the Right Wing Republican Party (with the dominant Tea Party faction) we now have. Neither was Eisenhower a tax cutter and, and in the main, he didn't try to reduce or repeal the New Deal programs.

No Big Tax Cutters Until President Reagan

In general, Eisenhower did not want to eliminate the safety net and other programs and taxes of the New Deal. Neither did Presidents Richard Nixon or Gerald Ford. It is interesting that Eisenhower didn't reduce the marginal federal income tax rate from 91% during his eight-year presidency—rather it was Democratic President Jack Kennedy who reduced the marginal federal income tax rate from 91% to 70% (still high). It was only since the Reagan Administration, beginning in 1981, that the Republican Party became the party of sharp tax cutters, essentially benefiting the wealthy.

Changes in Democrats' Economic Policy

Ordinary Americans Left Much Less Represented by Democrats' Move to the Right

After Lyndon Johnson was president, Hubert Humphrey was pushed to divide delegates to the next Democratic Convention into specific groups—so many women, so many African Americans, etc. One problem was that this essentially left out blue collar workers, a huge group who became the Reagan Democrats, helping to make Reagan so unbeatable in presidential elections. The change in strategy was from the universal benefits to the special interest benefits proved to be a weak political approach for the Democrats.

It seemed to me that Bill Clinton ran as a semi-FDR. He stressed he would help the "forgotten" middle class, and promised a middle-class tax cut. However, after he was elected, he said that the US couldn't afford the middle-class tax cut. He did say that he would be a "Third Way" president and was pro-business and especially pro-Wall-Street. During his administration, he essentially deregulated Wall Street. He said that he was pro-union, but did seemingly little to help them—though the unions were heavy campaign contributors and gave Bill Clinton a great deal of help in the form of union members as assistance in his "ground game."

Both Presidents (and former governors) Bill Clinton and Jimmy Carter were members of the Democratic Leadership Council (DLC), a group founded by Southern Democratic Governors to stop the bleeding of Democratic politicians—and voters—from the Democrats to the Republicans. A major difference from the former Democratic Party is that the new DLC was financed by business. It not only was pro-business, it was anti-union.

Although Bill Clinton did more for the real wages of the middle class than the Republicans did, he didn't really change the trends. As mentioned, his deregulation of Wall Street was also a major factor in the financial disaster that happened in a relatively short time after he helped deregulate it. This led to the Great Recession with its high unemployment, underemployment, and low wages, and a sharp rise in Income Inequality.

The Clinton Expansion a Boost to Average Americans — and to the Wealthy Even More

During the Bill Clinton economic expansion (1993–2000), American workers fared better than they had during the Bush expansion (2002–2006). Throughout the Clinton expansion, the median income of the bottom 99% increased by 2.4% a year in real dollars, much higher than the 0.9% per year they increased during the Bush expansion. However, during the Clinton expansion, the top 1% increased its income by 10.1% a year, more than three times as much as the percentage increase in income of the bottom 99%, and little different from the 11.0% per year increase they experienced during the Bush expansion (Wolfensohn 2010).

I believe that Barack Obama has an economic philosophy that is closer to Bill Clinton's than to Lyndon Johnson's, even though Obama passed the Affordable Care Act, often called "ObamaCare." (President Bill Clinton attempted to pass a universal healthcare bill as well, but failed.) However, I also believe that it is the leadership of the Democratic Party that has moved to the Right. I think there is a good chance that the base of the Democratic Party is still essentially liberal.

Deregulation of Economy Begun by Democratic Presidents Carter and Clinton

Both Carter and Bill Clinton—especially Clinton—deregulated the economy a great deal, especially those laws pertaining to Wall Street. For example, Clinton repealed the Glass-Steagall Act (which prevented banks from using government-guaranteed bank deposits to make (often risky) "bets" for themselves. President Bill Clinton's administration also allowed banks to reduce the amount of capital they were required to maintain within the bank. This allowed the banks to sharply increase their profits temporarily, but soon was a significant factor in the subsequent financial failure.

Because of these actions—and those of Republican Presidents Ronald Reagan and George W. Bush—the Great Recession ensued, speeding up the erosion of the middle class and damaging the very large majority of other ordinary Americans.

Higher Profits Versus Real Growth of Companies— and "Economic" Patriotism

From the short-term point of view, lowering labor costs is a high-probability way to increase corporate profits. On the other hand, it is necessary to take chances (invest in R&D and reinvest in the company) to really grow the company. Short-term thinking for the sake of raising immediate corporate profits and the stock price can often prove harmful in the long-term. Most important, lowering labor costs as a political strategy is the opposite of "economic" patriotism for the middle class and other ordinary Americans.

Republican Presidents Reagan and Bush Not "Economic" Patriots

It is ironic that the two presidents who seemed to scream "patriotism" from the rooftops, Ronald Reagan and George W. Bush, were "flag-waving" patriots but they weren't "economic" patriots, certainly not for the middle class and other ordinary Americans. They "talked the talk" but didn't "walk the walk." They simply didn't put their money where their mouths were.

Part VI

Some Possible Solutions

CHAPTER 14
A Permanent Jobs Department

CHAPTER 15
US Workers Need Representation in Negotiations with Management

CHAPTER 16
Vital: A Middle-Class Organization

CHAPTER 17
What Would the Middle-Class Organization Do?

Chapter 14

A Permanent Jobs Department

On Developing Good New Jobs in the US

This section examines a critical subject: how the US creates and sustains new, well-paying jobs. First, let's see what two well-known CEOs—Jeffrey Immelt and Andy Grove—have said about the subject.

Jeffrey Immelt, CEO of General Electric

Jeffrey Immelt, the CEO of the giant General Electric, who had been named by President Obama to lead a part-time commission on how to increase jobs and exports, was interviewed by Lesley Stahl in 2011 on the television show *60 Minutes* (CBS News 2011). One of the reasons Obama chose Immelt was that GE had brought back some manufacturing jobs from China and Mexico and was building factories in the US. However, GE's effort was on a small scale compared with what is needed for this country. Some key excepts from the interview are provided here:

Stahl: "We need to create 300,000 jobs a month, just to get back to where we were before the recession."

Immelt: "I think, Lesley, there needs to be a sense of national urgency around jobs that basically, if you just looked at how many hours a day do Republicans spend on job creation, do Democrats spend on job creation, and does the White House, it's nowhere close to 100%. We're not spending enough time on jobs."

Stahl: "If the Republicans say the government shouldn't spend, how the heck are we going to get ourselves out of this?"

Immelt: "No, no, this notion that the government has no role has never been true in the history of the United States. You know, really, all of the commercial aviation industry has grown out of defense spending. All of the health care innovation has grown out of the NIH (National Institutes of Health)."

Immelt: "We ought to be percolating twenty $1 billion businesses all the time that grow inside our system."

Also, Immelt has refocused his company on manufacturing, bulking up units like transportation, energy, and research and development. As the "Jobs Czar," he's urging his fellow CEOs to double their hiring of engineers and devote more money to R&D. At GE, he's tripled spending on everything from medical research to green technology.

Here are four points and suggestions from Immelt on US job creation:

1. The jobs problem is the worst it has been since the Great Depression. Yet, there is little time or energy spent on understanding the US jobs problem and how to solve it.
2. Many on the Right Wing are against the government spending money and say that the government doesn't know how to do anything except fight wars. Immelt replies that throughout our history, the government has been responsible for many key innovations that have greatly helped the private sector.
3. He urges his fellow CEOs to double their hiring of engineers and devote more money to R&D. At GE, Immelt is doing even more than that.
4. The US should have an industry percolator that would include 20 $1 billion industries at a time which fit into our system.

Great ideas! Can you imagine if the US had a permanent department of Immelt-like (but former) CEOs working full-time on this subject of jobs? For a long time, there has been a group of formerly successful small business owners that counsel others owning small businesses. Why not establish a department of (successful) former CEOs and top management to develop ideas on how to create more good jobs for Americans and make the US more economically productive? And why not make it a permanent department?

One concept would be for recent CEOs to do this full-time—people like Andy Grove, who we speak about next. I think that lots of former CEOs and other high-level former executives miss their work and would like to be able to help their country in this manner. Of course, the department would need people in other areas as well—marketing, advertising, research, etc. However, I stress the former CEOs and other high-level former executives because their experience would be invaluable.

Andy Grove, CEO of Intel

The Underlying Problem Isn't Simply Asian Costs

Probably the most insightful article I read in my research was the *Bloomberg Business* article by Andy Grove entitled "How America Can Create Jobs" (Grove 2010). Andy Grove is the co-founder and 19-year head of Intel, the huge high-tech company. Grove led the company to its huge growth. Since then, he has done a great deal of thinking in his retirement. Grove says: "The underlying problem isn't simply lower Asian costs. It's our own misplaced faith in the power of startups to create U.S. jobs. Americans love the idea of the guys in the garage developing something that will change the world." But what happens after that?

Scaling Is the Key to Jobs in Electronics

What Grove has to offer is that only 10% of the jobs created by a new product are in the innovation, while 90% of the jobs are in scaling. Scaling is a combination of getting a product ready for manufacture and the manufacturing itself. Not only production jobs are in scaling. There are lots of engineers and others involved in scaling. The huge electronic companies like Apple, Dell, etc. have 10% of its jobs in the US, while 90% are in China. The growth of this industry is more likely to solve the Chinese unemployment problem than the US unemployment problem.

Giving up Commodities Reduces Innovation

New York Times columnist Thomas Friedman recently encapsulated this innovation as the key view in his column: "Start-Ups, Not Bailouts" (Friedman 2010). His argument is that the US should allow commodity products to die if they have to. If we want to really create jobs, we should back start-ups. Grove continues, "Friedman is wrong. Start-ups are a wonderful thing, but they cannot by themselves increase tech employment. Equally important is what comes after that mythical moment of creation in the garage, as technology goes from prototype to mass production. This is the phase where companies scale up.... The scaling process is no longer happening in the U.S."

Yet, if you give up manufacturing the commodity, in a short time you often give up innovation in the area.

Manufacturing Is Where You Learn to Innovate

Also, manufacturing is where you learn to innovate. This goes beyond high tech, for example:

- Photo-voltaic parts (used in alternative energy): This type of high energy application was developed in the US, but we gave up on manufacturing them so we relinquished both the innovation and production to the Asian countries.
- Advanced batteries: Used in electric cars, these were also developed in the US. We gave up on their manufacturing and subsequently lost both the scaling and the innovation in this area.

Does Government Have a Place in Manufacturing?

The rapid development of Asian economies provides numerous illustrations. In a thorough study of the industrial development of East Asia, Robert Wade of the London School of Economics found that these economies turned in precedent-shattering economic performances over the 1970s and 1980s in large part because of the effective involvement of the government in targeting the growth of manufacturing industries.

Share of Profits versus Share of Market

Personally, I would describe this dynamic somewhat differently: We look for share of profits while the Asian countries look for share of market. The former leads to greater short-term profits and a higher stock price, while the latter leads to the long-term thinking that results not only in more good jobs, but also in true growth and further innovation.

The Significance of Scaling

"The first task is to rebuild our industrial commons. We should develop a system of financial incentives: Levy an extra tax on the product of offshore labor. (If the result is a trade war, treat it like other wars—fight to win.) Keep that money separate. Deposit it in the coffers of what we might call the Scaling Bank of the US. and make these sums available to companies that will scale their American operations. Such a system would be a daily reminder that while pursuing our company goals, all of us in business have a responsibility to maintain the industrial base on which we depend—on whose adaptability and stability we may have taken for granted." Grove believes that the underlying dynamics that have led us away from manufacturing have produced the current belief in the US that the only worthwhile jobs are information jobs—and the lack of prestige in manufacturing jobs.

Manufacturing Matters—a Lot!

Ironically, I read a book called *Manufacturing Matters* in the 1980s on just this topic—probably the most important of the more than 100 books I have read in this area of my research (Cohen 1988). We hope that by today America has also discovered the importance of manufacturing. Really, the US should look up to manufacturing, not down.

I am reminded of a statement by Ross Perot, the businessman who ran for president on a third party line and received 19% of the votes—and might even have won if he wasn't seen as an eccentric, if not worse. At the time, there was a lot of talk about old and new industries. Ross Perot, who was exceptionally smart, said he would like to develop a "new" industry—shoe manufacturing. Perot didn't mean just a shoe industry; he meant creating new industries which would provide lots of jobs, new or old, for America. He was agreeing with Andy Grove's job-centric approach (Grove's term).

Recently, I heard a very interesting analysis of the US problem regarding good jobs. A few decades ago, when the job market was healthy, the largest US company was General Motors, whose jobs paid $50 an hour (including benefits, and calculated in today's money) (Barnard 2004). Today, the US's largest employer is Walmart, whose full-time workers make an average of about $13 an hour, with part-time workers earning an average of $10 an hour (Isidore 2015). But it doesn't end there. I recently read another article about Walmart's drive to hire more part-time workers as a way to further cut down on benefits, and perhaps wages, too.

Areas of Study for the Jobs Department

The Automobile Industry Success Story

The US has a major big-industry success story in terms of finding out a problem and then fixing it. The US auto industry was falling apart. General Motors had once been the largest auto company in the world, and Chrysler was a second example of a highly successful American auto company. But both had fallen into terrible shape.

Most on the Right felt the two companies ought to be allowed to go bankrupt. Why throw good money after bad? However, President Obama was loath to do this. Between the assembly plants, the parts companies, the showrooms, etc., these companies comprised about one million jobs—the loss of such a large number of jobs didn't make much sense in the midst of the deep recession we were experiencing.

How It Was Achieved

The companies were not given bailout funds to spend as they liked. President Obama appointed a commission that would help identify the problems and how to fix them. What they found was that management was ossified—they simply could not make good, timely decisions—and the workers were paid wages and benefits that were too high to make the companies competitive.

Everybody made sacrifices (the CEO of General Motors left, for example), but the result was competitive car companies in a thriving American automobile industry. All those jobs were saved, and even some new ones were developed.

Could the Same Approach Have Worked in Finance?

One wonders why this approach wasn't used in the financial area as well. Instead, we allowed those who had caused the financial disaster to continue running the world of finance, and soon they were giving themselves the same gigantic bonuses they gave themselves before they caused the economic catastrophe—probably triggered, at least partly, by these often inappropriate, massive bonuses.

Can Other Industries Be Developed or Saved?

Considering the examples of the auto and financial industries, one can't help asking the question: Are there other industries that could and should be saved? I suspect so, and it would be the work of the new Jobs Department to find out which ones and where. It would also be the job of the Jobs Department to develop some ideas on new industries that would benefit the US most to enter.

Benchmarking for Real-World Results

A decade ago, I was doing some research on American healthcare, when a friend at a large American multinational company asked me to explain my approach. I told him that I was comparing the results of US healthcare to those of other advanced countries on important healthcare variables. Otherwise, how would I know how high is up? He laughed and told me that I was using a technique very popular in business, called "benchmarking."

Product Benchmarking Examples

1. The Xerox Case History

One of the early successes of benchmarking was at Xerox, which was in a bad way. The company decided to benchmark its brand and processes against the Japanese copier companies, which were the most successful in the world. Xerox learned that their Japanese competitors sold their copiers at the same price it took Xerox to manufacture them. By learning the approaches used by its world-class competitors, Xerox was able to identify their problems and fix them. Xerox became successful again, and the US still has a successful copier industry.

2. The Taurus Case History

Another success story is the building of a car by Ford. The company brought together 50 automobiles manufactured throughout the world and examined their best features in order to develop the Ford Taurus, which turned out to be the most successful car in the world for a number of years.

No doubt, there are other US products and services that can use benchmarking with world-class companies to improve performance.

Country Benchmarking Examples

Products are not the only category that can be benchmarked. The systems of a country can be benchmarked as well. I think that it would be useful to benchmark the US with the Netherlands, Germany, and even Singapore.

1. The Netherlands

The Netherlands has been called the "basket case" of Europe. Recently, its rate of sick leave and permanent disability were very high despite soaring exports and large gas reserves. The problem was even given a name: the Dutch disease (W. 2014). Everybody agreed that something had to be done if the Netherlands were to become a thriving country again. Its companies needed more flexibility, and the unions negotiated with the companies, with the government acting as the referee. The results were very useful. The workers agreed to a great deal of part-time jobs. Actually, many women liked the idea. They could work and also spend more time with their children.

On the other hand, the changes weren't made on the backs of the workers. For example, even the part-time workers had healthcare insurance. The Netherlands significantly improved its economy. It is more efficient. There is better morale. And the Netherlands has a strong economy now.

2. Germany

I believe it would be very useful to benchmark the US versus Germany, a very economically successful country. Germans get lots of paid vacation time, sick leave, and maternal leave, and Germany has an excellent universal healthcare system. And Germany manages to have one of the top two trade surpluses in the world and has been able to continue manufacturing by going into advanced engineering, which isn't easily outsourced. Germany also has an excellent apprentice system. This may be one of its real strengths.

As mentioned earlier, Jeffrey Immelt, who headed a committee to learn how the US could increase exports, concluded that one major reason why the US doesn't do well in trade is that American companies don't try very hard to export (Malone 2011). On the other hand, Immelt pointed Germany out as a country that plays for keeps in exporting, and claims this is a reason it is so successful. I am sure that the US could learn a lot from benchmarking Germany.

3. Singapore

Of course, Singapore is a tiny country compared to the US. The reason I think it may be useful for the US to benchmark (or at least study) Singapore is that it is the only country I have come across in my research that is not only successful but takes actions that specifically aim to reduce Income Inequality.

American Exceptionalism: An Unworkable Concept

Note that the American companies in the product benchmarking examples compared their products and services to their world-class competitors, evidence that as US companies are aware that those elsewhere often produce superior products and sometimes use more efficient processes than the US does.

American companies can't afford the commonly heard ideological bias of American Exceptionalism. As mentioned earlier, it's easy to claim that "the US has the best healthcare in the world," but this is nonsense. Not only does the US spend twice as much per capita as the average advanced country using a universal healthcare system, but quite a few of these other countries have better outcomes than the US.

For example, unlike the countries providing universal healthcare, the US has 30 million people who don't have healthcare insurance. A 2009 research study from Harvard estimated that about 45,000 Americans die every year because they lack healthcare insurance. This is in addition to probably hundreds of thousands or even millions who don't get timely medical care, allowing their existing medical conditions get worse because of cost. In the countries with a universal healthcare system, everyone has healthcare insurance, so this problem of people getting sicker—or even dying—because they lack healthcare insurance isn't a problem.

The Future of Manufacturing

Can Manufacturing Succeed in the US?

There is essential agreement that the US needs more manufacturing, which has a strong multiplier effect (it also introduces other good jobs along with it). Insufficient manufacturing has long been a US problem. Indeed, the central section of the US, in which much of American manufacturing used to take place, is often called the "rust belt."

How do some countries keep up with manufacturing and maintain its good jobs? For example, how did Germany successfully go into advanced engineering, which is very difficult to outsource? The Jobs Department could find this out.

Can We Bring Manufacturing Jobs Back?

Our big multinationals used to offer the US's best jobs. But they now provide millions fewer jobs in the US and millions more jobs in other countries. Have we been successful in bringing some jobs back? I think so. Can we learn from these examples? Probably.

The Internet has been a major factor in the job market—the US government was in fact responsible for much of the development of the computer and the Internet. Are our schools well set up for this? Can we do a better job here?

The "Permanent Disabilities" Problem: Simply a Function of Difficulty Finding Jobs?

The US is experiencing a growing issue with permanent disabilities, and the percentage of disabled men in the workforce has been decreasing for years. This is a problem that could be researched by the Jobs Department, which could use the experience of other countries, especially those countries that have solved this issue, as I believe the Netherlands has. There is the feeling on the part of some that "permanent disabilities" has become a problem because it is difficult for the so-called "permanently disabled" to find a good job or possibly any job at all.

Our Educational System: Prepared for the Job Market Ahead?

Is our educational system set up well for the near-term and far-term job markets? How can we do a better job in education for blue collar jobs? Perhaps Germany is successful in advanced engineering because of the way they train manufacturing workers. We won't know unless we closely study the situation. Should fewer Americans go to college and more learn a trade? If yes, how can this best be done? Let's study countries that have been successful in doing this.

Chapter 15

US Workers Need Representation in Negotiations with Management

On its face, American workers should be shouting for unions. When unions were strong, about 35% of workers in the private sector were unionized, and the US grew the largest middle class in the history of the world. Then, many single-earner families could live a middle-class life style, whereas today, many two-earner families often live paycheck to paycheck. Indeed, it's difficult to call some of these families "middle class" even though they consider themselves as such.

The Unwritten Contract: Its Significance and Eventual Termination

The collapse of the union movement caused major problems even among non-union workers. When the union movement was strong, companies feared that dissatisfied non-union workers might join or even form their own union. As a result, many companies acceded to an unwritten contract where they treated non-union workers well. When they no longer had to worry about workers joining a union, they tended to end the unwritten contract.

The Taft-Hartley Bill and the End of the Closed Shop

It was the Taft-Hartley bill passed by Congress over the veto by President Harry Truman that ended the closed shop (the need to pay dues to a union accepted by a majority of the workers who negotiated for pay and benefit raises, pensions, etc.) so workers could receive the fruits of the labor of the union, without paying dues. This made union organizing impractical in the so-called "right to work" states, because it costs a lot of money to organize and run a union.

The Common American View of Unions:
Favorable but No Longer Relevant

Most Americans are in favor of unions being able to negotiate wages and benefits for the worker. In a March 2011 poll, respondents were asked "Do you think workers in this country should or should not have a right to form unions to negotiate with employers on issues like working conditions, pay, benefits, and pensions? No fewer than 81% said they should, compared to 18% who said they should not. In similar polls, the results have been less dramatic, but a majority of Americans (usually more than 60%) think that workers should have a right to be represented by a union (Washington Post/ABC News 2011).

However, most believe that unions are a thing of the past, and that they will be weaker in 10 years than they are today. And some Americans, despite feeling helpless on the job, are against unions altogether. The reason they feel helpless is because no one represents them in negotiations with management; management's motivation, on the other hand, is to lower labor costs in order to increase corporate profits, the stock price, and eventually, their compensation. Also, unions have been considerably demonized by expensive propaganda.

Worker Representation in Management Negotiations
in the US versus Other Countries

It is useful to compare the US to other advanced countries in union and non-union (e.g., works councils, company-wide, industry-wide) coverage with management, as is seen in Table 12:

Table 12
Percentage of Worker Representation
(Unions or Non-Unions) by Country

	Union coverage %	Non-union coverage %	Total coverage %
Austria	38	61	99
Finland	71	2	95
France	8	87	95
Sweden	82	10	92
Netherlands	29	53	82
Spain	16	65	81
Norway	56	21	77
Germany	27	36	63
Australia	23	27	50
United Kingdom	29	6	35
Japan	20	14	34
Canada	30	2	32
United States	13	1	14
(Average-non-US)	36	34	70
US-private sector	7	0	7

Table 12 is illuminating. In advanced countries other than the US, an average of 36% of workers have union coverage, and 34% have negotiating rights, though not through a union. An average total of 70% of workers have negotiating rights.

On the other hand, in the US, only 7% of workers in the private sector are covered by a union, and it appears that few have negotiating rights without unions. In other words, workers in other countries with advanced economies are 10 times as likely as American workers in the private sector to have negotiating rights with management (70% to 7%).

The Struggle to Organize Workers under Today's Labor Laws

With today's labor laws, it is very difficult to organize a private company when top management is against it—and they are usually very much against it. Popular union-suppression tactics that companies frequently employ today are:

- Firing pro-union employees until the remaining employees lose their enthusiasm to organize.

- Litigating the contract for a long time whenever a union has won a majority of employees who vote to be represented by the union. Some unions win an election, but it seems to take forever for them to get a contract because of perpetual "negotiations."

- Hiring labor consultants who specialize in "union busting" and union prevention.

- Unfavorable rulings on union claims by the generally employer-favoring National Labor Relations Board (NLRB)—usually appointed by a Republican president.

- Employers often use unfair labor tactics. However, until the National Labor Relations Board rules against them and they are fined, whatever the employers have done is a fait accompli; they have done the job they have set out to do—in other words, scare the workers. The fine is considered by the employer as a reasonable cost of doing business.

A good tactic that the average American can use to regain power in negotiations with management is through labor law reform, which would make it possible for a majority of workers to organize a company without threats of harassment—sort of a new Wagner Act. But how to get the American people to back labor law reform, especially when organized labor/unions have been so demonized by opponents?

The Challenge: Changing American Minds about Unions

Two studies show both the potential for unions and their current significant weakness in the minds of Americans:

- In his well-received book, *One Nation After All*, Alan Wolfe reports that the middle class "is growing increasingly hostile to corporations," which suggests the potential for unions. Wolfe reports, however, that the middle class "is indifferent to unions" (Wolfe 1998). This is a troublesome paradox for union organizers.

- There is a similar paradox in a September 1997 poll conducted by Princeton Research and sponsored by PBS and *USA Today*. The study shows that American workers are having significant problems in the workplace: 59% say they have to work harder today to make a decent living than they used to, while only 15% say they have to work less hard, and 73% report more on-the-job stress. These findings represent significant discontent among working Americans.

Yet other responses in the study indicate that Americans do not consider unions as an option. By a nearly three to one margin (68% to 24%), Americans think that unions will be weaker 10 years from now than today. This feeling that "unions are not the future" is a major obstacle that unions must overcome.

I've had a lot of experience in my commercial life conducting studies with new products and services, sometimes in turnaround situations. I have found that the key to success is to find product dissatisfactions and/or unsatisfied needs with the currently available products or services.

First, to get the average American to want to join a union and to desire labor law reform, unions have to show that a strong labor movement will help them make more money, receive more benefits, obtain more and better jobs, and get more peace of mind on the job. Some examples:

- Show that average Americans got their fair share of productivity and prosperity when unions were strong, but have suffered since unions have weakened. When unions were strong, the US developed the largest middle class in the history of the world. When unions eroded, so did the US middle class.
- Remind average Americans of the basic advantages of union membership:
  - Union employees earn more than non-union workers.
  - Union workers get better benefits.
  - Union workers can only be fired for cause.
  - 90% of union members are glad they belong to a union, so why wouldn't a very high percentage of new members be glad to be union members?

I believe that a well-thought-through, heavy advertising and public relations campaign could make union fans of average American workers. One example of the potential of advertising and promotion for unions is that a union campaign beat the "payroll protection" (an anti-union approach) referendum in California even though more than 70% of voters favored it when the unions began their campaign.

However, advertising has to create an image that is different from—and better than—the way unions are currently being communicated. Up to this moment, unions have been highly vilified, commonly viewed as a bunch of thugs who smoke fat cigars and make companies uncompetitive.

Advertising must communicate an entirely new twenty-first-century union. And specifics must be included. I also believe it is important to show that a strong union movement and higher wages, benefits, and pensions would be excellent for the US economy. It would be a good idea to communicate that the US economy is not a supply-side but a demand-side economy, and higher wages, lower unemployment, and underemployment would mean that the US would become a much healthier consumer market again—companies would once again see the US as a great growth economy and increase investment in their US operations.

Based on a great deal of experience in research, I believe the resurgence of unions could take place effectively. American workers today feel helpless on the job, and aren't happy about the situation. Workers have little or no power today on the job, but a strong union movement could give it back to them.

Through unions, they would once again be represented in negotiations with management. Workers would no longer have to accept the whims of management, including the need to significantly lower labor costs simply to increase the short-term stock price and the CEO's and top management's compensation.

One problem often raised as an obstacle to strengthening unions again is that jobs today are very different than they once were, and impervious to unionization. However, we should remember that years ago, the AFL (American Federation of Labor—the union movement of the time, essentially made up of skilled workers), felt it wouldn't be practical to try to organize unskilled workers. Yet, those unskilled workers—assembly-line workers, steel workers, etc.—became the backbone of the huge CIO (Congress of Industrial Organizations). Eventually, the two union organizations came together as the AFL-CIO.

A new union movement would undoubtedly have to make adjustments. But the fact remains that most workers have a great need for representation in negotiations with management for wages, benefits, pensions, etc. Today, companies have a huge advantage when negotiating with workers, if one can even call them negotiations. As a result, workers are getting a raw deal on the job, resulting in Income Inequality.

$20 an Hour for Fast-Food Workers? Really?

Earlier, we described a recent *New York Times* article that described how a Danish fast-food worker earns $20 an hour for a 40-hour week and benefits a US fast-food worker could only dream about.

How is this possible?

There is no law on the matter, but all Danish fast-food workers belong to the 3F union and $20 an hour is the pay bargained for with the employer organization. What the employers get is peace—the agreement to no strikes, demonstrations, or boycotts.

McDonald's learned about this the hard way. When it came to Denmark in the 1980s, it refused to join the employer's association or adopt any collectively bargained agreements. Only after nearly a year of raucous, union-led protests did McDonald's relent.

Actually, the Danish workers don't really earn $20 an hour in American dollars because the Danish cost-of-living is 30% higher than in the US, bringing the wage to $14 an hour in US dollars; and Denmark is a high-tax country (Alderman and Greenhouse 2014). What is most important, however, is that Danish fast-food workers earn a living wage. Tell me, are unions important for workers?

Unions Can Play Hardball

One last point before I leave this chapter: in political election after political election, unions are the biggest campaign contributors to the Democratic Party and its candidates, and make available to the candidates thousands of union members for the "ground game," reaching and persuading voters to vote for Democratic candidates and getting them to the polls. Yet, the Democrats seem to do little to nothing about getting labor law reform even considered. I am only one person (though experienced in marketing and marketing research), but I wouldn't give the Democrats—or any other party—a dime until they agreed to fight for labor law reform. I hypothesize that when they see they won't get money or people power, the Democrats will agree to work to pass union reform. They can, in many ways.

Chapter 16

Vital: A Middle-Class Organization

This chapter explores the creation of a nonpolitical, nonpartisan Middle-Class Organization (MCO) to represent American workers.

The American Middle-Class: Many Voters but Little Political or Economic Power

The middle class and those who aspire to become middle class have serious economic problems. While they are a substantial majority of Americans (and voters), with 47% seeing themselves as middle class and an estimated 10% (my estimate) who aspire to the middle class, for a total of about 60% of American voters, they have little political power, which translates into little economic power. (To a major degree, the bottom 99% can serve our purposes here, instead of the middle class in particular.)

The Democratic Party: From Middle-Class Representative to Wall Street Supporter

The Middle Class Once Championed by Democrats

The Democratic Party—from Franklin D. Roosevelt in 1932 to Lyndon Baines Johnson in 1968—did essentially represent the middle class. Even Dwight Eisenhower, the lone Republican president during that Democratic president run, did not try to repeal the social and safety net programs set up by Franklin Roosevelt and the three other Democratic presidents that followed. And Eisenhower, a real conservative president, was not a tax cutter. He said he wouldn't cut taxes until the US paid off its debts. When Eisenhower became president, the marginal federal income tax was 91%, and by the time he left eight years later, it was still 91%.

The Switch to a Losing Special Benefit Strategy

But the Democratic Party strategy changed radically. In the chaos of the 1968

Democratic convention, Hubert Humphrey had to agree to a change in the process of selecting delegates. So many had to be minorities, so many had to be women, etc. A special disaster was that there was no quota for blue collar workers, who then became the Reagan Democrats. Essentially, the strategy of the Democratic Party changed from being a universal benefit party (nearly all Americans reach the age of 65) to being a special interest benefit party. They found it to be a losing strategy.

Another Strategy Switch to the "Third Way"

The next Democratic president to be elected was Bill Clinton, who used a very different strategy. He called himself a follower of the 'Third Way," but he was really a centrist, triangulating between the objectives of the Democratic and Republican Parties. He was both pro-middle-class and pro-business.

In any case, using the Third Way strategy, the Democratic Party would find it difficult to take action that would hurt business and the wealthy, even if it helped the middle class.

The Middle Class versus the Wealthy under Clinton

The middle class and other ordinary Americans managed reasonably well economically (in real wages) in the Bill Clinton recovery, but the wealthy (top 1%) fared much better. Their incomes increased by more than three times the rate of increase of the median worker. Also, there are at least two other important points worth making here:

- Bill Clinton did little or nothing about labor law reform, and unionization continued to plummet, offering workers less and less representation and power.
- The Bill Clinton administration was very friendly to business, especially to Wall Street. The Glass-Steagall Act, preventing banks from using government-guaranteed savings for their own "bets," was repealed, and the leverage ratio was sharply reduced, allowing banks to risk much more money for their own purposes. The downside was that banks could reserve significantly less money as capital for protection, which could and did have a disastrous effect.

FDR's Protective Regulations Repealed by Clinton

The protections of Main Street from Wall Street afforded by the regulations put in place by President Roosevelt kept the US financial situation safe for more than 60 years. However, President Bill Clinton essentially deregulated Wall Street, and about 10 years later, the financial disaster of 2008 struck. The Great Recession followed.

Roosevelt's versus Obama's Post-Financial Disaster Strategy

There were major differences between the ways the Roosevelt and the Obama administrations acted after the two financial disasters. President Roosevelt led a public investigation to discover what had caused the financial disaster. As a result, he made changes that safeguarded the financial industry. For example, he set up the Securities and Exchange Commission (SEC) to control Wall Street, and the Glass-Steagall Act, which didn't allow banks to "bet" bank deposits guaranteed by the government for their own accounts. He also began the Federal Deposit Insurance Corporation (FDIC), paid for by the banks, which stopped "bank runs."

The Obama administration, on the other hand, did very little to investigate what caused the financial disaster. At least, nobody on Wall Street or in the big banks was indicted. In fact, Obama appointed many of the individuals who caused the financial problems to financial posts within his administration. (In contrast, hundreds of executives had been indicted and hundreds went to jail in the Savings and Loan scandal in the 1980s.) Popular terms used in the new financial disaster were "too big to fail" and "too big to jail." Instead, the big banks were bailed out. They seemed to have no shame for what they had done and were soon giving themselves huge bonuses like they did before. Crime had paid—and well.

"Third Way" Democratic Presidents—Giving Wall Street Its Way

While a good personality in the Democratic Party could win the presidency with the "Third Way" strategy (like Bill Clinton and Obama did), being president with this strategy didn't mean what it once did. Unlike the Franklin Roosevelt and Lyndon Johnson administrations, which represented the middle class and other ordinary Americans, the Bill Clinton administration acted on behalf of big business, especially Wall Street, as much as for ordinary Americans. Also, Bill Clinton and Obama received much of their campaign contributions from Wall Street—and so has Hillary Clinton, who has defended Wall Street in her speeches, for which she was paid hundreds of thousands of dollars.

Someone put it well: the Democratic Party moved from the left to the middle while the Republican Party moved to the Insane Asylum. There are no more moderate Republicans, and the Democrats no longer represent only the middle class and other ordinary Americans.

Republican Party Tax Cuts and Other Attempted Legislation

With Reagan and Bush, a Sharp Republican Move to the Right

The Republican Party had shifted sharply to the Right, starting especially with Ronald Reagan, who cut the marginal federal tax rate (paid by the wealthy) from 70% to 28% (by 60%) and also some of the financial income taxes. He also made the famous, very Right Wing quote: "Government is not the solution to our problem; government is the problem."

Then, George W. Bush cut taxes for the wealthy by a great deal more. He lowered the marginal federal income tax from 39.6% to 35% (Bill Clinton had increased it from 31% to 39.6%), the Dividend tax from the regular federal income tax rate (39.6%) to 15%, and reduced the estate tax sharply, disparaging its very nature by calling it the "death tax" when it is really a wealth tax, best measured when a person dies.

Due to influence of the Tea Party, the Republican Party has progressed much further to the Right. And the party continues moving from the center-right to the far right of the Tea Party, which has come to dominate it—at least in ideology and voting behavior.

George W. Bush's Attempt to Privatize Social Security

George W. Bush also tried to privatize Social Security by proposing that those with Social Security invest in the stock market. This would have been a disaster if it had passed and become law, as it was soon followed by the financial crack-up in which most Americans would have lost half or more of their Social Security money. There is a rule in individual pension money, especially for retired individuals and those close to retirement: don't put your money in risky propositions. The people who would have gained in the Bush privatization would be in Wall Street—the stock brokers, mutual funds, etc.

Creating a Middle-Class Organization

Five Potential Concepts for a Middle-Class Organization

Following are five approaches we explored for an organization that would help the middle class, an organization that could help turn around Income Inequality and get the middle class and other ordinary Americans their fair share of American prosperity.

1. **The Democratic Party.** My first thought was the Democratic Party. After all, the Democratic Party brought many social and safety net programs to the US, and the American people have come to show great appreciation for these programs. However, as mentioned earlier, the Democratic Party has moved to the Right and cannot be expected to stop, let alone turn around Income Inequality.

   I have analyzed the political changes of the political parties, especially the Democratic Party, to show that one cannot expect the Democratic Party to turn around Income Inequality. Very simply, the Democratic Party receives its campaign contributions from similar places as the Republican Party, especially Wall Street.

2. **The Middle Class as a Third Political Party**. Although polling suggests that the American people would be sympathetic to a third party, I don't believe this would work. A middle-class third party wouldn't work because it would be in the same "swamp" as the other political parties, requiring money from people and companies who want something in return.

3. A Middle-Class Blog. A middle class blog would take a long time to work—if at all. The Internet is a wondrous place, but not if you want to develop an organization in a timely fashion. That "everything" is on the Internet means that unless your audience is looking for it, a large number of people won't find it. A middle class blog could be useful, but not as the central tactic here.

4. A Nonprofit Middle-Class Think Tank. As with the middle-class blog, a nonprofit middle-class think tank might work to some degree, but not as the central thrust.

5. An Approach I Believe Would Work: A Nonprofit, Nonpolitical Middle-Class Organization. While I was still considering a middle-class think tank (though not optimistically), I asked my son Alan what he thought about the situation—what did he think might work? He answered my question with another: "What nonprofit organization was I aware of that very successfully helped a specific demographic?" I immediately realized what he was getting at.

The American Association of Retired People (AARP), with millions of members, has developed a great deal of political power. Trying to make changes in the entitlements (especially Social Security, Medicare, and Medicaid) has been called the "third rail" of American politics. Other than when the Greenspan Commission solved a money shortage problem, the two major political parties haven't "touched the third rail" except to add a pharmaceutical benefit program for seniors and Medicaid. Well, there are far more Americans who see themselves as middle class, aspiring to enter the middle class, or just ordinary Americans than there are seniors.

Politicians will need the votes of an effective Middle-Class Organization and will act accordingly.

The Middle-Class Organization Should Be Nonpolitical

A warning: I don't think the Middle-Class Organization should take on essentially political issues. Rather, it should stick to economic issues, regarding which the middle class is treated unfairly, or may be in the future. In this way, it would act as the AARP does. Most seniors vote Republican, yet they do well receiving big government programs—and many millions of Republicans are fans of the AARP. The AARP doesn't act as a blue state or a red state. Rather, it serves as a "green" group, taking actions that will positively affect seniors economically.

The Middle-Class Organization should act in a similar manner. It should be remembered that more than two-thirds of Tea Party members and sympathizers want Medicare (and probably Social Security) to remain as it is. So, it's important that the Middle-Class Organization be seen as nonpolitical. If money and benefits are the sole issues involved, ordinary Democrats and Republicans—even those who favor the Tea Party—should approve of the organization.

Chapter 17

What Would the Middle-Class Organization Do?

Of course, this section is written based on a single person's analysis (my own) of the data. There will certainly be changes when the organization is actually developed and in working order.

First, it is important that the Middle-Class Organization (MCO) be nonpolitical. This is essential because, for one, it will allow members of all political parties—and Independents—to join the organization, as individuals across the entire political spectrum use government programs. For example, two-thirds of the Tea Party would like Medicare to remain as it stands, even though some wouldn't have guessed this from the extreme Right regarding a Big Government organization. Similarly, the AARP is a large organization created for the assistance of seniors, yet seniors tend to vote Republican. I don't think the AARP would have been nearly as successful if it were political. If the MCO stays nonpolitical, it can help people of all political persuasions. Instead of functioning like a red or blue state, it would base its actions on what it can do for its members. Following are a number of key issues the Middle-Class Organization could take on for middle class and other ordinary Americans.

1. First, I would like to name four benefits that all, or nearly all, people in the other advanced countries enjoy but which people in the US lack. For three of the four, I wasn't even aware before I did this research that any countries had these benefits:

    a. Paid vacation leave by law: The US is the only country in the world with an advanced economy that doesn't have a minimum amount of paid vacation days leave per year by law.

    b. Paid sick leave by law: Nearly all other advanced countries in the world have a minimum number of paid sick days leave by law, but not the US. The result is that 40% of American workers don't get any paid sick leave at all from their job.

    c. Paid parental (maternal/paternal) leave by law: Most advanced countries—other than the US—offer by law a minimum number of days (averaging 17 weeks) of paid parental leave after a baby is born.

    d. Universal healthcare by law: Aside from the US, all the other advanced countries in the world (and many non-advanced countries) have universal healthcare by law. For tens of millions of Americans, paying for healthcare is a burden. Nearly 43 million Americans have a medical debt, and a medical debt is one of the three major reasons Americans go into bankruptcy (Kristof 2014). There are few or no medical debts in these other advanced countries, so medical debts don't lead to bankruptcy.

2. Wouldn't Americans lead a much improved life if they were guaranteed substantial vacation and sick leave (with a long leave for a serious illness), maternal leave when a baby is born, and guaranteed medical care if a family member became ill? Americans would also have fewer debts, less worry, and much more peace of mind.

3. The government guarantees these benefits, but often the company must pay for them. It is no wonder that American companies hire lobbyists to fight these benefits and make campaign contributions to congressmen who vote against them.

4. American companies say they can't afford to pay for these benefits, that it would make them uncompetitive in the global economy. But this is not the case. The fact that other advanced countries pay for these benefits does not indicate that they have any problem competing in the global economy. In fact, these countries have a substantial trade surplus with the US. It is actually the US that has by far the largest trade debt in the world.

5. One other related point: American multinational companies pay for these benefits for their workers in these other advanced countries, and I have never come across information stating they are having trouble doing so—or even complained about doing so. My explanation for these dynamics is cynical. It is that the US CEOs don't want to pay for these benefits because they want to maximize the corporate profits of the company and the stock price, which would ultimately maximize their reputations and compensation.

6. The MCO would fight for these important benefits for middle-class and other ordinary Americans, and would be able to offer strong arguments. And, of course, when the MCO is more mature, there is a good chance it would obtain enough votes to acquire the political power necessary to make desired changes, leading to economic power. Politicians want to get reelected, and they need enough votes with which to do it. Politicians would need the votes of the Middle-Class Organization members, and would act accordingly.

7. This book names and discusses the root causes of Income Inequality, as well as what we believe to be a practical solution to this problem—creating a nonprofit, nonpolitical Middle-Class Organization. Again, the MCO could develop enough power to be an important voice in the debate on important public issues. It is also important for the American people and American politicians to have this information (for example, the type of information in this book), so the organization could effectively communicate it.

8. We have discussed why workers are hurting even though corporate profits and stock prices are soaring in this weak economy. The knowledge that companies are withholding earnings that used to go to them would upset many workers, but they would now have an organization with the power to do something about it.

9. This book presents 10 tax myths that make the rich richer. It also explains why they are myths, and then clarifies the truths. A solution would be to lower the total taxes of the middle-class and other ordinary Americans, and to increase the total taxes of the wealthy. This is because the middle class pays almost as high a total tax rate as the rich, and our economic history suggests that taxes could be much more progressive than they are.

10. It's clear that while 50% more Americans say they are conservative as say they are liberal, Americans appreciate—even love—the Big Government programs they have been provided, and would be against any changes in them, let alone have them repealed, even though many politicians on the Right want to reduce or repeal them.

11. It is important that the MCO make people aware of the services already available to them through the government so they will be open to other benefits that would significantly improve their lives—and which the US can afford.

12. The middle class should be shown that Social Security is not only an extraordinarily important program to the American people but that it is by no means a financial problem. Even those politicians who say they are concerned about its finances admit that the program can pay full benefits for the next 18 years without making any changes. Indeed, it is possible that the program may never require a reduction of benefits, increase in the eligibility age, etc. It should also be noted that millions of Social Security beneficiaries are very low-income individuals, even with the current Social Security benefits, and cannot afford to have a cut in benefits. Another point against changes is that the program is helpful during difficult economic times, since Social Security beneficiaries tend to spend the benefits they receive quickly, which helps our demand-side economy. In any case, what is the rush to reduce the Social Security program?

13. This book discusses how many of the traditional economic measures are no longer relevant in the change from a Business Economy to a *Stock Price Economy*. To replace these, we've presented new statistics that should work well in the new *Stock Price Economy*.

14. The book shows that the US economy currently benefits the wealthy and suggests whom it should work for if it functions properly. Currently, Main Street is losing the battle with Wall Street. It makes more sense for Wall Street to reflect Main Street.

15. It is assumed by many that soaring stock market indexes indicate a strong economy. This used to be the case in the Business Economy, when the Stock Market reflected the economy. However, in this *Stock Price Economy*, the soaring stock market indexes can be indicative of a weak economy, with companies siphoning off income that used to go to workers but now goes to increasing corporate profits and a high stock price.

16. The book divides the concept of patriotism into two very different types: "flag-waving" patriotism and "economic" patriotism. Too often, the politicians who scream patriotism from the roof-tops are "flag-waving" patriots, but not "economic" patriots. They don't put their money where their mouth is. The American people need to know and understand the two very different kinds of patriotism and which politicians fall into which category.

17. The MCO would set up a Jobs Department to determine how to create and keep good (high-paying) jobs for the US. This would include a study of which countries have succeeded in this regard, and see if this leads to insights on how this can be achieved in the US. The benchmarking analytic technique, much used by business, would be very useful in this regard.

18. The MCO would look to develop representatives for workers in the negotiations with top management for pay, benefits, pensions, etc. Many American workers tend to feel helpless on the job, as it is not realistic for an individual worker to negotiate with a CEO. The representation could be in the form of unions, works councils, etc. Other approaches are possible as well. Again, further study would be needed.

The above list offers potential ideas for the MCO. No doubt, there will be others to be determined by the organization as it develops.

Bibliography

Alderman, Liz, and Steven Greenhouse. 2014. "Living Wages, Rarity for U.S Fast-Food Workers, Served Up in Denmark." *The New York Times*, October 27.

American Heritage Foundation. 2016. "Explore the Data." *2016 Index of Economic Freedom*. Accessed February 2, 2016. http://www.heritage.org/index/explore.

—. 2015. "Top 10 Percent of Earners Paid 68 Percent of Federal Income Taxes." *2015 Federal Budget in Pictures*. Accessed February 23, 2016. http://www.heritage.org/federalbudget/top10-percent-income-earners.

Barber, Elizabeth. 2014. "George H.W. Bush honored for courage with 1990 tax hikes." *Reuters*. May 4. Accessed February 22, 2016. http://www.reuters.com/article/us-usa-kennedy-bush-idUS BREA4308G20140505.

Barnard, John. 2004. *American Vanguard: The United Auto Workers During the Reuther Years, 1935-1970*. Detroit: Wayne State University Press.

Barry-Jester, Anna, and Ben Casselman. 2015. "33 Million Americans Still Don't Have Health Insurance." *FiveThirtyEight*. September 28. Accessed February 1, 2016. http://fivethirtyeight.com/features/33-million-americans-still-dont-have-health-insurance/.

Bivens, Josh, Elise Gould, Lawrence Mishel, and Heidi Shierholz. 2014. "Raising America's Pay: Why It's Our Central Economic Policy Challenge." *Economic Policy Institute*. June 4. Accessed February 2, 2016. http://www.epi.org/publication/raising-americas-pay/.

Book, Robert. 2013. "In Other Countries, Everyone Has Access To Health Care." *Forbes*.

Bresiger, Gregory. 2014. "According to the Fed, the rich are getting richer." *New York Post*. November 2. Accessed February 23, 2016. http://

nypost.com/2014/11/02/according-to-the-fed-the-rich-are-getting-richer/.

Brownstein, Ronald. 2003. "Bush Breaks With 140 Years of History in Plan for Wartime Tax Cut." *Los Angeles Times*. January 13. Accessed February 22, 2016. http://articles.latimes.com/2003/jan/13/nation/na-outlook13.

Burger, Rachel. 2014. "Why Your Unpaid Internship Makes You Less Employable." *Forbes*.

CBS News. 2011. "The Jobs Czar: General Electric's Jeffrey Immelt." *60 Minutes*. October 9. Accessed February 26, 2016. http://www.cbsnews.com/news/the-jobs-czar-general-electrics-jeffrey-immelt/.

Cecere, David. 2009. "New study finds 45,000 deaths annually linked to lack of health coverage." *Harvard Gazette*. September 17. Accessed February 24, 2016. http://news.harvard.edu/gazette/story/2009/09/new-study-finds-45000-deaths-annually-linked-to-lack-of-health-coverage/.

Center for Economic and Policy Research. 2012. "Germany Has Outperformed the U.S. Because of Work Sharing." *Beat the Press*. October 25. Accessed February 2, 2016. http://cepr.net/blogs/beat-the-press/germany-has-outperformed-the-us-because-of-work-sharing.

Center on Budget and Policy Priorities. 2015. "Policy Basics: Where Do Our Federal Tax Dollars Go?" *Research*. March 11. Accessed February 23, 2016. http://www.cbpp.org/research/policy-basics-where-do-our-federal-tax-dollars-go.

Center on Budget and Policy Priorities. 2015. "Policy Basics: Where Do Federal Tax Revenues Come From?" *Center on Budget and Policy Priorities: Research*. March 11. Accessed February 22, 2016. http://www.cbpp.org/research/policy-basics-where-do-federal-tax-revenues-come-from.

Chapman, Jeff, and Michael Ettlinger. 2005. "Social Security and the income of the elderly." *Economic Policy Institute.* April 4. Accessed February 24, 2016. http://www.epi.org/publication/ib206/.

Clinton, William. 1996. "Address Before a Joint Session of the Congress on the State of the Union." *The American Presidency Project.* January 23. Accessed February 22, 2016. http://www.presidency. ucsb.edu/ws/?pid=53091.

Cohen, Stephen S. 1988. *Manufacturing Matters: The Myth of the Post-Industrial Economy.* Basic Books.

Congressional Budget Office. 2009. "Table 1: Distribution of Federal Taxes and Household Income." *Historical Effective Federal Tax Rates: 1979 to 2006.* April. Accessed February 25, 2016. https://www.cbo. gov/sites/default/files/111th-congress-2009-2010/reports/effective_ tax_rates_2006.pdf.

Cooke, Kristina. 2011. "Reuters." *Most Americans say tax rich to balance budget: poll.* January 3. Accessed February 22, 2016. http://www. reuters.com/article/us-usa-taxes-poll-idUSTRE7022AK20110103.

Cornerstone Wealth Management, LLC. 2011. "Measuring Inflation: How Government Has Changed the Yardstick." *Cornerstone Wealth Management.* April. Accessed February 2, 2016. http://www. cornerstonewm.com/downloads/measuring-inflation.pdf.

Cronin, Brenda. 2013. "Some 95% of 2009–2012 Income Gains Went to Wealthiest 1%." *Wall Street Journal.* September 10. Accessed February 25, 2016. http://blogs.wsj.com/economics/2013/09/10/ some-95-of-2009-2012-income-gains-went-to-wealthiest-1/.

Delaney, Arthur. 2010. "Two-Thirds Of Americans Support Raising Minimum Wage: Poll." *HuffPost Politics.* October 6. Accessed February 24, 2016. http://www.huffingtonpost.com/2010/10/06/ americans-minimum-wage-poll_n_752921.html.

DeNavas-Walkt, Carmen, Bernadette D. Proctor, and Jessica C. Smith. 2013. "Income, Poverty, and Health Insurance Coverage in the United States: 2012." *Census.gov.* September. Accessed February 2, 2016. http://www.census.gov/prod/2013pubs/p60-245.pdf.

Desilver, Drew. 2015. "5 facts about Social Security." *Pew Research Center.* August 18. Accessed February 23, 2016. http://www.pewresearch. org/fact-tank/2015/08/18/5-facts-about-social-security/.

Dubay, Curtis S. 2013. "The Bush Tax Cuts Explained: Where Are They Now?" *The Heritage Foundation.* February 20. Accessed February 22, 2016. http://www.heritage.org/research/reports/2013/02/ bush-tax-cuts-explained-facts-costs-tax-rates-charts.

Eichelberger, Erika, and Dave Gilson. 2015. "How US Companies Stash Billions Overseas—Tax-Free." *Mother Jones.* February 6. Accessed February 23, 2016. http://www.motherjones.com/politics/2015/02/ foreign-overseas-tax-inversion-evasion-obama.

Eisenhower, Dwight D. 1954. "Social Insecurity." *Snopes.* November 8. Accessed February 26, 2016. http://www.snopes.com/politics/ quotes/ikesocial.asp.

Farley, Robert. 2012. "Dependency and Romney's 47 Percenters." *FactCheck. org.* September 18. Accessed February 22, 2016. http://www. factcheck.org/2012/09/dependency-and-romneys-47-percenters/.

—. 2012. "Does Romney Pay a Lower Rate in Taxes Than You?" *FactCheck.org.* August 3. Accessed February 22, 2016. http://www. factcheck.org/2012/08/does-romney-pay-a-lower-rate-in-taxes- than-you/.

Federal Reserve Board. 2014. *Changes in U.S. Family Finances from 2010 to 2013: Evidence from the Survey of Consumer Finances.* Bulletin, Washington DC: Federal Reserve.

Fisher, Max. 2012. "Here's a Map of the Countries That Provide Universal Health Care (America's Still Not on It)." *The Atlantic.*

Fowler, Meg. 2011. "From Eisenhower to Obama: What the Wealthiest Americans Pay in Taxes." *ABC News.* January 24. Accessed February 22, 2016. http://abcnews.go.com/Politics/eisenhower-obama- wealthy-americans-mitt-romney-pay-taxes/story?id=15387862#2.

Friedman, Thomas. 2010. "Start-Ups, Not Bailouts." *The New York Times.*

April 3. Accessed February 26, 2016. http://www.nytimes.com/2010/04/04/opinion/04friedman.html?_r=0.

Goss, Stephen C. 2010. "The Future Financial Status of the Social Security Program." *Social Security Administration*. Accessed February 24, 2016. https://www.ssa.gov/policy/docs/ssb/v70n3/v70n3p111.html.

Gould, Elise. 2014. "Why America's Workers Need Faster Wage Growth— And What We Can Do About It." *Economic Policy Institute*. August 27. Accessed January 1, 2016. http://www.epi.org/publication/why-americas-workers-need-faster-wage-growth/.

Graham, David A. 2013. "How a Small Team of Democrats Defeated Larry Summers—and Obama." *The Atlantic*. September 15. Accessed February 24, 2016. http://www.theatlantic.com/politics/archive/2013/09/how-a-small-team-of-democrats-defeated-larry-summers-and-obama/279688/.

Green, Joshua. 2001. "Meet Mr. Death." *The American Prospect*. December 19. Accessed February 24, 2016. http://prospect.org/article/meet-mr-death.

Greenhouse, Steven. 2013. "Fighting Back Against Wretched Wages." *The New York Times*, July 27.

Greider, William. 1981. "The Education of David Stockman." *The Atlantic*, December.

Gross, Bill. 2004. "Haute Con Job." *Investment Outlook* (www.pimco.com).

Grove, Andy. 2010. "How America Can Create Jobs." *Bloomberg Business*.

Hall, Kevin G. 2011. "Strong corporate profits amid weak economy - What's up with that?" *McClatchyDC*. March 27. Accessed February 1, 2016. http://www.mcclatchydc.com/news/nation-world/national/economy/article24618424.html.

Harris, John F. 2010. "Bill Clinton: The sequel." *Politico*. September 24. Accessed February 25, 2016. http://www.politico.com/news/stories/0910/42661_Page5.html.

Hirsch, Barry T. 2011. "Unions, Dynamism, and Economic Performance." *Research Handbook on the Economics of Labor and Employment Law*. Accessed February 1, 2015. http://lawcha.org/wordpress/century-teaching-organizing/.

Ingraham, Christopher. 2015. "More than a third of American workers don't get sick leave, and they're making the rest of us ill." *The Washington Post*, January 15.

Isidore, Chris. 2013. "Buffett says he's still paying lower tax rate than his secretary." *CNN Money*. March 4. Accessed February 22, 2016. http://money.cnn.com/2013/03/04/news/economy/buffett-secretary-taxes/.

—. 2015. "Walmart ups pay well above minimum wage." *CNN Money*. February 19. Accessed February 26, 2016. http://money.cnn.com/2015/02/19/news/companies/walmart-wages/.

Johnston, Katie. 2014. "Nearly 1 in 4 US workers go without paid time off." *Boston Globe*, August 14.

Kane, Jason. 2012. "Health Costs: How the U.S. Compares With Other Countries." *PBS NewsHour*. October 12. Accessed February 22, 2016. http://www.pbs.org/newshour/rundown/health-costs-how-the-us-compares-with-other-countries/.

Kantor, Jodi. 2014. "Working Anything but 9 to 5." *The New York Times*, August 13.

Kocieniewski, David. 2011. "G.E.'s Strategies Let It Avoid Taxes Altogether." *The New York Times*. March 24. Accessed February 23, 2016. http://www.nytimes.com/2011/03/25/business/economy/25tax.html.

Kristof, Kathy. 2014. "43 million Americans burdened with medical debt." *CBS Money Watch*. December 11. Accessed February 26, 2016. http://www.cbsnews.com/news/haphazard-system-scars-43-million-americans-with-medical-debt/.

Krugman, Paul. 2009. "Reagan Did It." *The New York Times*. May 31.

Accessed February 25, 2016. http://www.nytimes.com/2009/06/01/opinion/01krugman.html.

Kucinich, Jackie, and Kevin McCoy. 2012. "Romney releases taxes, claims he has paid every year." *USA Today*. September 12. Accessed February 22, 2016. http://usatoday30.usatoday.com/news/politics/story/2012/09/21/romney-taxes/57821564/1.

Kurtzleben, Danielle. 2015. "Lots Of Other Countries Mandate Paid Leave. Why Not The U.S.?" *NPR*. July 15. Accessed February 1, 2016. http://www.npr.org/sections/itsallpolitics/2015/07/15/422957640/lots-of-other-countries-mandate-paid-leave-why-not-the-us.

Lach, Alex. 2012. "5 Facts About Overseas Outsourcing." *Center for American Progress*. July 9. Accessed February 1, 2016. https://www.americanprogress.org/issues/labor/news/2012/07/09/11898/5-facts-about-overseas-outsourcing/.

Langlois, Shawn. 2015. "Tim Cook says this is the real reason Apple products are made in China." *MarketWatch*. December 21. Accessed February 1, 2016. http://www.marketwatch.com/story/tim-cook-apple-doesnt-make-its-products-in-china-because-its-cheaper-2015-12-20.

Lazonick, William. 2014. "Profits Without Prosperity." *Harvard Business Review*, September.

—. 2011. "Nine Government Investments That Made Us an Industrial Economic Leader." *HuffPost* Business. September 8. Accessed February 24, 2016. http://www.huffingtonpost.com/william-lazonick/nine-government-investmen_b_954185.html.

Leonhardt, David. 2012. *The New York Times Economix Blog*. August 20. Accessed January 20, 2015. http://economix.blogs.nytimes.com/2012/08/20/the-14-potential-causes-of-the-income-slump/.

Liberto, Jennifer. 2012. "Offshore havens saved Microsoft $7B in taxes - Senate panel." *CNN Money*. September 20. Accessed February 23, 2016. http://money.cnn.com/2012/09/20/technology/offshore-tax-havens/.

Lincoln, Abraham. 1863. *Transcript of the Gettysburg Address*. November 19. Accessed February 22, 2016. http://rmc.library.cornell.edu/gettysburg/good_cause/transcript.htm.

Long, Heather. 2015. "What the heck is the controversial Glass-Steagall Act?" *CNN Money*. October 14. Accessed February 24, 2016. http://money.cnn.com/2015/10/14/investing/democratic-debate-what-is-glass-steagall-act/.

MacroTrends. 2016. *Dow Jones 100 Year Historical Chart*. February 2. Accessed February 2, 2016. http://www.macrotrends.net/1319/dow-jones-100-year-historical-chart.

Malone, Scott. 2011. "U.S. not "trying that hard" on exports - GE's Immelt." *Reuters*. October 17. Accessed February 2, 2016. http://uk.reuters.com/article/uk-ge-immelt-idUKTRE79G2R920111017.

Manuel, Dave. 2016. *Inflation Calculator*. Accessed February 22, 2016. http://www.davemanuel.com/inflation-calculator.php.

Market Watch. 2016. "Watch America's student-loan debt grow $2,726 every second." *MarketWatch.com*. January 30. Accessed February 23, 2016. http://www.marketwatch.com/story/every-second-americans-get-buried-under-another-3055-in-student-loan-debt-2015-06-10.

Martin, Patricia P., and David A. Weaver. 2005. "Social Security: A Program and Policy History." *Social Security Office of Policy*. Accessed February 24, 2016. https://www.ssa.gov/policy/docs/ssb/v66n1/v66n1p1.html.

Mauboussin, Michael J. 2012. "The True Measures of Success." *Harvard Business Review*.

McBride, William. 2012. "Romney, Obama, & Simpson-Bowles: How Do the Tax Reform Plans Stack Up?" *Tax Foundation*. September 6. Accessed February 25, 2016. http://taxfoundation.org/article/romney-obama-simpson-bowles-how-do-tax-reform-plans-stack.

Mellon, Andrew. 1924. *Taxation: The People's Business*. New York: The MacMillan Company. https://archive.org/stream/taxation thepeopl033026mbp/taxationthepeopl033026mbp_djvu.txt.

Mishel, Lawrence, Elise Gould, and Josh Bivens. 2015. "Wage Stagnation in Nine Charts." *Economic Policy Institute*. January 6. Accessed February 25, 2016. http://www.epi.org/publication/ charting-wage-stagnation/.

Molyneux, Guy. 2010. "Hart Research Associates Poll on Continuing Unemployment Benefits." *National Employment Law Project*. November 15. Accessed February 25 2016, 2016. http://www.nelp. org/content/uploads/Me10105.pdf.

Morris, Jim, and Chip Mitchell. 2012. "Temps: America's Throwaway Workers." *Mother Jones*.

NELP. 2014. "Tracking the Low-Wage Recovery: Industry Employment & Wages." *National Employment Law Project*. April 27. Accessed February 2, 2016. http://www.nelp.org/publication/ tracking-the-low-wage-recovery-industry-employment-wages/.

Nisen, Max. 2013. "Caterpillar CEO: 'We Can Never Make Enough Profit'." *Business Insider*. May 17. Accessed February 2, 2016. http://www. businessinsider.com/caterpillar-ceo-quote-on-workers-2013-5.

Nisen, Max. 2013. "GE CEO Jeff Immelt: Here's The Case For Making Things In America Again." *Business Insider*.

Oak, Robert. 2012. "The Rich and the Rest of Us in the United States." *The Economic Populist*. September 12. Accessed February 23, 2016. http://www.economicpopulist.org/content/rich-and-rest-us- united-states.

Obama, Barack. 2013. "Remarks by the President on Economic Mobility." whitehouse.gov December 4. Accessed January 20, 2015. https: //www.whitehouse.gov/the-press-office/2013/12/04/remarks- president-economic-mobility.

ObamaCare Facts. 2012. "ObamaCare Poll: ObamaCare Approval Rating Popularity." *ObamaCare Facts*. Accessed February 24, 2016.

http://obamacarefacts.com/obamacare-poll/.

OECD. 2016. "Revenue Statistics - provisional data on tax ratios for 2014."
Organisation for Economic Cooperation and Development.
Accessed February 22, 2016. http://www.oecd.org/ctp/tax-policy/
revenue-statistics-ratio-change-latest-years.htm.

—. 2014. "Society at a glance: Coverage for health care." *OECD iLibrary.*
Accessed February 22, 2016. http://www.oecd-ilibrary.org/sites/
soc_glance-2014-en/06/05/index.html?contentType=%2fns%2f-
Chapter%2c%2fns%2fStatisticalPublication&itemId=%2fcontent%
2fchapter%2fsoc_glance-2014-26-en&mimeType=text%2fhtml&-
containerItemId=%2fcontent%2fserial%2f19991290&acces-
sItemIds=.

On the Issues. 2012. "Tea Party on Social Security." *On the Issues.* Accessed
February 22, 2016. http://www.ontheissues.org/Celeb/Tea_Party_
Social_Security.htm.

O'Toole, James. 2013. "GAO: U.S. corporations pay average effective tax rate
of 12.6%." *CNN Money.* July 1. Accessed February 23, 2016. http:
//money.cnn.com/2013/07/01/news/economy/corporate-tax-rate/.

Paletta, Damian. 2012. "With Tax Break, Corporate Rate Is Lowest in
Decades." *The Wall Street Journal.* February 3. Accessed February
26, 2016. http://www.wsj.com/articles/SB10001424052970204662
04577199492233215330.

Palmer, Karen S. 1999. "A Brief History: Universal Health Care Efforts in
the US." *Physicians for a National Health Program.* Accessed
February 24, 2016. http://www.pnhp.org/facts/a-brief-history-
universal-health-care-efforts-in-the-us.

Pew Research Center. 2007. "Daily Number: April 18, 2007." *Pew Research
Center.* April 18. Accessed February 25, 2016. http://www.
pewresearch.org/daily-number/think-environmental-laws-and-
regulations-should-be-stricter/.

—. 2007. "Daily Number: May 25, 2007." *Pew Research Center*. May 25. Accessed February 25, 2016. http://www.pewresearch.org/ daily-number/think-corporate-profits-too-high/.

—. 2015. "Most Say Government Policies Since Recession Have Done Little to Help Middle Class, Poor." *U.S. Politics & Policy*. March 4. Accessed February 2, 2016. http://www.people-press.org/2015/03/04/most-say-government-policies-since-recession-have-done-little-to-help-middle-class-poor/.

—. 2012. "Partisan Polarization in Bush, Obama Years, Section 5: Values About Business, Wall Street and Labor." *Pew Research Center*. June 4. Accessed February 24, 2016. http://www. people-press.org/2012/06/04/section-5-values-about-business-wall-street-and-labor/.

Pomerleau, Kyle. 2014. "The Missing Business Tax Revenue in Corporate Tax Data." *Tax Foundation*. April 17. Accessed February 26, 2016. http: //taxfoundation.org/blog/missing-business-tax-revenue-corporate-tax-data.

Ray, Rebecca, Milla Sanes, and John Schmitt. 2013. "No-Vacation Nation Revisited." *Center for Economic and Policy Research*. Accessed February 22, 2016. http://cepr.net/documents/publications/no-vacation-update-2013-05.pdf.

Reagan, Ronald. 1981. "Inaugural Address." *The Ronald Reagan Presidential Foundation & Library*. January 20. Accessed February 22, 2016. http://www.reaganfoundation.org/reagan-quotes-detail. aspx?tx=2072.

—. 1987. "State of the Union Address." *ThisNation.com*. January 27. Accessed February 22, 2016. http://www.thisnation.com/library/ sotu/1987rr.html.

Resnikoff, Ned. 2014. "How Tenn. politicians killed Volkswagen unionization." *MSNBC*. April 4. Accessed February 25, 2016. http: //www.msnbc.com/msnbc/tennessee-volkswagen-chattanooga-union#51477.

Reuters. 2009. "Simmons mattress company is bankrupt, to be sold."
Reuters: Business. November 16. Accessed February 21, 2016. http://
www.reuters.com/article/us-simmons-idUSTRE5AF2X420091116.

—. 2016. "U.S. consumer spending flat; savings at three-year high." *CNBC.*
February 1. Accessed February 1, 2016. http://www.cnbc.
com/2016/02/01/us-personal-income-dec-2015.html.

Robertson, Lori. 2009. "Dying from Lack of Insurance." *FactCheck.org.*
September 24. Accessed February 1, 2016. http://www.factcheck.
org/2009/09/dying-from-lack-of-insurance/.

Romig, Kathleen. 2008. *Social Security Reform: Possible Effects on the
Elderly Poor and Mitigation Options.* Report, Washington D.C.:
Congressional Research Service.

Roosevelt, Franklin D. 1936. "Speech from Democratic National Convention."
Miller Center. June 27. Accessed February 2, 2016. http://
millercenter.org/president/speeches/speech-3305.

Roy, Avik. 2012. "The Tortuous History of Conservatives and the Individual
Mandate." *Forbes.* February 7. Accessed February 24, 2016. http://
www.forbes.com/sites/theapothecary/2012/02/07/the-tortuous-
conservative-history-of-the-individual-mandate/#638f9770597a.

Russell Sage Foundation. 2012. "Real Mean and Median Income, Families
and Individuals, 1947-2012, and Households, 1967-2012." *Chartbook
of Social Inequality.* Accessed February 23, 2016. http://www.
russellsage.org/sites/all/files/chartbook/Income%20and%20
Earnings.pdf.

Saad, Lydia. 2010. "Americans Unsure About "Progressive" Political
Label." *Gallup.* July 12. Accessed February 24, 2016. http://www.
gallup.com/poll/141218/americans-unsure-progressive-political-
label.aspx.

Saez, Emmanuel. 2013. Striking it Richer: *The Evolution of Top Incomes in
the United States.* Academic Paper, Berkeley: UC Berkeley.

Sahadi, Jeanne. 2010. "Taxes: What people forget about Reagan."

CNN Money. September 12. Accessed February 22, 2016. http://money.cnn.com/2010/09/08/news/economy/reagan_years_taxes/.

Sargent, Greg. 2011. "'There's been class warfare for the last 20 years, and my class has won'." *The Washington Post.* September 30. Accessed February 22, 2016. https://www.washingtonpost.com/blogs/plum-line/post/theres-been-class-warfare-for-the-last-20-years-and-my-class-has-won/2011/03/03/gIQApaFbAL_blog.html.

Shierholz, Heidi, and Lawrence Mishel. 2011. "The sad but true story of wages in America." *Economic Policy Institute.* March 15. Accessed January 1, 2016. http://www.epi.org/publication/the_sad_but_true_story_of_wages_in_america/.

Shlaes, Amity. 2015. "Why the Flat Tax Is More Popular Than Ever." *Time.* November 10. Accessed February 22, 2016. http://time.com/4107231/flat-tax/.

Social Security Administration. 2009. "Fast Facts & Figures About Social Security, 2009." *Social Security: Office of Retirement and Disability Policy.* Accessed February 23, 2016. https://www.ssa.gov/policy/docs/chartbooks/fast_facts/2009/fast_facts09.html#generalinfo.

—. 2015. "Old-Age and Survivors Insurance Trust Fund, 1937-2014 ." *Social Security.* Accessed February 22 2016, 2016. https://www.ssa.gov/oact/STATS/table4a1.html.

—. 2015. "Social Security Basic Facts." SSA *Press Office.* October 13. Accessed February 23, 2016. https://www.ssa.gov/news/press/basicfact.html.

—. 2016. "Your Unanswered Questions...Answered." *Open Government Initiative.* Accessed February 23, 2016. https://ssa.gov/open/webinar-questions-and-answers.html.

Sorkin, Andrew Ross. 2013. "Obligations and Motivations in the Battle for Dell." *The New York Times,* March 25.

Stone, Chad, and Sherman Arloc. 2010. "Center on Budget and Policy Priorities." *Income Gaps Between Very Rich and Everyone Else*

More Than Tripled in Last Three Decades, New Data Show.
June 25. Accessed January 20, 2015. http://www.cbpp.org/research/
income-gaps-between-very-rich-and-everyone-else-more-than-
tripled-in-last-three-decades-new.

Tau, Byron. 2012. "Obama sparred with Steve Jobs over outsourcing."
Politico. January 21. Accessed February 21, 2016. http://www.
politico.com/blogs/politico44/2012/01/obama-sparred-with-steve-
jobs-over-outsourcing-111751.

Tax Foundation. 2013. "U.S. Federal Individual Income Tax Rates History,
1862-2013 (Nominal and Inflation-Adjusted Brackets)."
Tax Foundation. October 7. Accessed February 22, 2016. http://
taxfoundation.org/article/us-federal-individual-
income-tax-rates-history-1913-2013-nominal-and-inflation-
adjusted-brackets.

The Commonwealth Fund. 2015. "U.S. Health Care from a Global
Perspective." *The Commonwealth Fund.* Accessed February 24,
2016. http://www.commonwealthfund.org/publications/
issue-briefs/2015/oct/us-health-care-from-a-global-perspective.

The Heritage Foundation. 1981. "Reagan's First Inaugural: "Government is
not the solution to our problem; government is the problem.".""
First Principles Series. January 20. Accessed February 24, 2016.
http://www.heritage.org/initiatives/first-principles/primary-
sources/reagans-first-inaugural-government-is-not-the-solution-
to-our-problem-government-is-the-problem.

The Kaiser Commission on Medicaid and the Uninsured. 2015. "Key Facts
about the Uninsured Population." *The Kaiser Family Foundation.*
October 5. Accessed February 22, 2016. http://kff.org/uninsured/
fact-sheet/key-facts-about-the-uninsured-population/.

The Kaiser Family Foundation. 2005. *National Survey of the Public's Views
About Medicaid.* Survey, Menlo Park: The Kaiser Family Foundation.

The Laffer Center. 2014. "The Laffer Curve." *The Laffer Center.*

Accessed February 25, 2016. http://www.laffercenter.com/the-laffer-center-2/the-laffer-curve/.

The World Bank. 2016. "GDP growth (annual %)." *The World Bank: Data.* Accessed February 15, 2016. http://data.worldbank.org/indicator/ NY.GDP.MKTP.KD.ZG.

—. 2015. "Household final consumption expenditure, etc. (% of GDP)." *The World Bank: Data.* Accessed February 21, 2016. http://data. world-bank.org/indicator/NE.CON.PETC.ZS.

Travisa. 2016. "Germany Travel Information." *Germany Visa.* Accessed February 25, 2016. http://germany.travisa.com/Country-Page.aspx?CountryID=DE.

Truman, Harry S. 1948. "Know Nothing, Do Nothing Congress." *Speeches USA.* October 7. Accessed February 25, 2016. http://www. speeches-usa.com/Transcripts/harry_truman-nothing.html.

U.S. Bureau of Labor Statistics. 2012. *Spotlight on Statistics: The Recession of 2007-2009.* February. Accessed February 1, 2016. http://www.bls. gov/spotlight/2012/recession/.

—. 2012. "The Recession of 2007-2009." *BLS Spotlight on Statistics.* February. Accessed February 2, 2016. http://www.bls.gov/ spotlight/2012/recession/pdf/recession_bls_spotlight.pdf.

—. 2012. "Unemployment Rates Around the World." *BLS Spotlight on Statistics: The Recession of 2007–2009.* February. Accessed February 2, 2016. http://www.bls.gov/spotlight/2012/recession/ data_ilc_unemployment.htm.

—. 2016. "Union Members Survey." *Economic News Release.* January 28. Accessed February 2 2016. http://www.bls.gov/news.release/union2. nro.htm.

U.S. Division of International Labor Comparisons. 2013. *International Unemployment Rates and Employment Indexes, Seasonally Adjusted, 2009-2013.* Statistical Analysis, Washington, D.C.: U.S.

Bureau of Labor Statistics.

U.S. Employee Benefits Security Administration. 1999. "Report of the Working Group on the Benefit Implications of the Growth of a Contingent Workforce." *U.S. Department of Labor.* November 10. Accessed February 1, 2016. http://www.dol.gov/ebsa/publications/contrpt.htm.

U.S. Government Accountability Office. 2015. "Contingent Workforce: Size, Characteristics, Earnings, and Benefits." April 20. Accessed February 2, 2016. http://www.gao.gov/products/GAO-15-168R.

U.S. Government Revenue. 2011. "Federal 2011 Taxes by Type." *Federal 2011 Government Revenue.* Accessed March 10, 2016. http://www.usgovernmentrevenue.com/fed_revenue_2011USrn.

Uchitelle, Louis. 1999. "The American Middle, Just Getting By." *The New York Times.* August 1. Accessed February 24, 2016. http://www.nytimes.com/1999/08/01/business/economic-view-the-american-middle-just-getting-by.html?pagewanted=all.

W., C. 2014. "What Dutch disease is, and why it's bad." *The Economist.* November 5. Accessed February 26, 2016. http://www.economist.com/blogs/economist-explains/2014/11/economist-explains-2.

Waldman, Paul. 2014. "Obama Compared to Prior Presidents On Job Creation, In Graphs." *The American Prospect.* December 21. Accessed February 22 2016. http://prospect.org/article/obama-compared-prior-presidents-job-creation-graphs.

Warren, Elizabeth, and Amelia Warren Tyagi. 2003. *The Two-Income Trap: Why Middle-Class Parents Are Going Broke.* Chicago: Basic Books.

Washington Post/ABC News. 2011. "Washington Post/ABC News Poll." *Polls.* March. Accessed March 10, 2016. http://www.washingtonpost.com/wp-srv/politics/polls/postpoll_03142011.html.

Wolfe, Alan. 1998. *One Nation, After All.* New York: Penguin.

Wolfensohn, James. 2010. *The Inequality Puzzle: European and U.S. Leaders Discuss Rising Income Inequality.* Berlin: Spring.

Woods Jr., Thomas E. 2009. "Kill the Monster." *The American Conservative.* July 13. Accessed February 22, 2016. http://staging. theamericanconservative.com/articles/kill-the-monster/.

www.ingramcontent.com/pod-product-compliance
Lightning Source LLC
Chambersburg PA
CBHW060030210326
41520CB00009B/1065